THE
WHITE
CAT

Musson, Dave (author)
The White Cat
978-1-922890-83-2
Self-Help

Typeset Minion Pro 11/15

Cover and book design by Green Hill Publishing

A guide in waking up to the truth; that you are.

THE WHITE CAT

DAVE MUSSON

ACKNOWLEDGEMENTS

I wish to acknowledge

Professor Dr. Satyanarayana Chillapa (Swamiji), Robert Becker, and Swami Atmachaithanya for your guidance on the yogic journey of spiritual development.

Mooji, Eckhart Tolle and Wayne Dyer for revealing so much of the pathway.

Rose Fegan and Kelly Brown for your spiritual accompaniment.

Abigail Wilson for your proof reading expertise.

All of the other friends and family that have some way shared in this journey and made this book possible.

A special acknowledgement must go to my greatest teacher: my beautiful wife Loren. You are not just an editor and compiler of this book, you are the essence of this book. Your grace fills my every day with divinity. You true self shines forth for all to see, always. A light that will certainly shine for all eternity.

"...we cannot do any religious, social, and spiritual activities without the sacred participation of wife which is called as 'Ardhangi' The-half of once body."

-Swamiji

First Print 2018

CONTENTS (BOOK ONE)

Acknowledgments iv
BOOK ONE:
  REVEALING YOUR TRUTH............................ X
Prologue... 1
Introduction 3
Chapter 1 ✷
  Being Human..7
Chapter 2 ✷
  Ego 12
Chapter 3 ✷
  Mind 17
Chapter 4 ✷
  Thoughts and Positive Thinking...................................23
Chapter 5 ✷
  Acceptance of What is / No Resistance 27
Chapter 6 ✷
  Attachment / Desires 31
Chapter 7 ✷
  Judgement 35
Chapter 8 ✷
  Breaking Free from Judging,
  Resisting and Attaching..39

Chapter 9 ✆
Acceptance of suffering 42
Chapter 10 ✆
The Now – Being present 46
Chapter 11 ✆
Being true to yourself by being your true self 50
Chapter 12 ✆
Mind/Ego Puts up a Fight 53
Chapter 13 ✆
Rest in peace 56
Epilogue ....
A day in the life of a Seer 59
Appendix A ....
Body Awareness 62
Breath Awareness 65
Meditation 68
Stillness Practice 70

CONTENTS (BOOK TWO)

BOOK TWO:
    CENTERING IN YOUR TRUE SELF 73
Introduction 75
Breaking free – My personal story 75
Chapter 1 ॐ
    Importance of guidance 81
Chapter 2 ॐ
    States of consciousness 86
Chapter 3 ॐ
    Witness consciousness 93
Chapter 4 ॐ
    Placing zero value in thoughts - The Golden Key 98
Chapter 5 ॐ
    Meditation and stillness 104
Chapter 6 ॐ
    Impermanence 111
Chapter 7 ॐ
    Balance 114
Chapter 8 ॐ
    Intuitive knowing 119
Chapter 9 ॐ
    Selfless intent 122

Chapter 10 ॐ
Non-labelling/no judgement Revisiting JAR............126
Chapter 11 ॐ
Equanimity...130
Chapter 12 ॐ
Fight the good fight– Giving thanks to suffering.....134
Chapter 13 ॐ
Surrender 138
Chapter 14 ॐ
Falling Down 142
Chapter 15 ॐ
Facing Fears 147
Chapter 16 ॐ
Recalling your power...150
Chapter 17 ॐ
Self-empowerment..153
Chapter 18 ॐ
Spiritual seeker - The false witness 157
Chapter 19 ॐ
Staying present 160
Chapter 20 ॐ
True love – Oneness..163
Glossary 167
Afterword 173
Personal Notes..178

Book One

REVEALING YOUR
TRUTH

PROLOGUE

T HIS BOOK SHOULD BE picked up and read whenever you have some spare time. Importantly though it should also be put down often too.

For it's when the book is put down that the true magic occurs. Taking a break creates space and opportunity for yourself to truly understand and 'feel' the ideas contained here.

However, you may decide to read this book through completely and then put it down for a while, before picking it back up some time later and reading a part again.

It's here for what you need most and at the time you need it most. It is purely a guide.

It will help you to eventually understand that you have ALL of the answers inside of you!

Much of the writings and understandings in this book will seem at times both extremely simple and yet quite complex. This is quite normal. As you will learn there is a part of you which feels that some of the ideas suggested in this book are natural and unquestionably true and another (mind-based) part of you which struggles to comprehend the very same information purely because it goes against

1

everything that it believes. This is ok. It is only human nature and therefore not personal.

Take as much time as you need with the book. Some parts of it will make an immediate impact. Others may plant a simple seed, which in the future may flourish to full understanding. It's your journey and it takes as long as it takes, so take your time and enjoy.

INTRODUCTION

T HERE IS SOMETHING INCREDIBLY peaceful about sailing on the open seas.

It's often the case that, when you reach a certain distance from any mainland, you can look in all directions to the horizon and all you see is air and water. The vast expanse of an ocean is visible to about 15km and as it meets the eternal sky it presents an almost mystical seam of perfect unison. As you scan the horizon looking for a sign of anything to tell you that you're not completely alone in this visible area stretching approximately 700km2, it starts to occur to you that your eyes, so used to being bombarded by *otherness*, are actually not deceiving you. Not a ship, outcrop of land or even a living creature in sight.

It can often take the mind a bit of time to comprehend and even accept this. But when it does and eventually it always will, a certain peace transcends and you are left often speechless and in wonderment. The human mind in any normal human living environment is usually surrounded by countless 'objects of attention' and yet here we find ourselves confronted by the shocking simplicity of just two objects, sky and sea.

This moment of silence is often brief. It is usually not too long before the mind goes from thinking of nothing, to starting to interpret even this most serene vision of simplicity. The mind loves to see separation and difference. It is still receiving the same pictures that the eyes have been sending the brain, but now it is translating them into a multitude of change. Waves, clouds, white tips of frothing water, colour variations in the blue of the sky.

It has taken the mind just a few seconds to dismantle a serene vision of nothingness and rearrange things into its own version of 'this and that'.

It may not be too long before the mind then begins to imagine what else is beyond the horizon or consider the seething aquatic activity below the surface. The mind is now starting to imagine things that cannot even be seen. It will not be too long before the mind drifts off again completely into its own little personal world of thoughts and the moment will be seemingly lost in a cloud of mental activity.

But a moment of silence did occur.

Now it may be that the vision was not an endless ocean, but a beautiful sunset, a starry night, or fields of flowing grass. It could even be a darkened room, the song of a bird, a ride on a bike or a refreshingly cool gust of wind on a hot day. It is something that is possible to a cell bound prisoner as well as a monk in a Himalayan monastery. Something in the simplistic beauty that life offered in this moment made you pause for the briefest of moments and the normal chattering mind subsided briefly and stillness remained. Amongst all the loud activity of the normal human mind, a gap occurred where it had nothing to offer. Life itself silenced it and you were there to witness it.

But who is this 'you' that witnessed it? If the *mind* was silent then how is it that you could be aware of this moment? Is it possible that you are not just what you think of all day long?

We shall begin to see that this 'perceiver' is who you are and it is consciousness itself. It is your true essence. It is free from past or future and therefore free from worry or fear. It is eternal and therefore not bound by the cycle of birth and death. It is blissful awareness. It is the *life of life* and it is available to you right here and right now.

So how do you begin to become aware of yourself, as this perfect stillness, free from all the suffering a mind-based human life can hold?

Well let us imagine that there was a path that lead to it. In fact, to be more accurate, the path actually becomes it. Then let us say in finding this book, whether it was on a shelf at a library, left on a train or given by a friend, you had suddenly found the path, or that possibly the path had found you.

So now you have a destination that appeals to you, a path to get there and hopefully, having read this far, a feeling like it is a you that you would like to be.

A *you* that is free. Free from all of your suffering.

If that is the case then the moment you found this book and began reading with an intent to learn more...your journey began. You took the first step.

Now you may ask how long is the path and how long will it take? Well this I cannot answer, but I can tell you, for some of you it will take no time at all and for others it will take longer. If you are in the latter group and it does take longer, that does not mean you are inferior or less in any way than someone who achieves the goal faster.

In fact, it may be that the longer it takes, the more you have to gain.

The Chinese philosopher Lao Tzu once said, "The journey of a thousand miles begins with one step." Your first step has been taken.

Let's continue the journey...

Chapter One

BEING HUMAN

I T HAS OFTEN BEEN said by the great Yogis of India that to be gifted the opportunity of a human life is one of the greatest of all gifts available in the Universe.

Why? You may ask, when it appears that so many humans around the planet appear to be suffering, be it mentally, emotionally, physically or a combination of all of these.

The reasoning of the enlightened gurus is our first example of a suggested truth both stunningly simple and yet seemingly complex. They state that a human life enables life to become aware of itself.

What does this mean? *Life* becomes aware of *itself*.

Well it is unquestionable that you have life within you, a fact you could not survive without. It is therefore quite easy to assume that all living things are gifted with life also. Now imagine for a moment that you incarnated onto this planet as the life in a tree instead of a human. You would have life but no mind to be perceptive of anything else. You would simply be a tree until the tree perished. Let us switch lives now and become a cat or a dog, you would now have a brain which can learn and make decisions, but you would have no capability of becoming aware of your own self.

The Yogis believe that the true gift of a human life is the ability to become *conscious* of your own self. As humans, we have the incredible ability to use the mind for much more than simple life-sustaining decisions, or attraction and aversion to desires and fears as does the dog, who bounds up to its owner when he grabs the leash for the evening walk or goes to hide after ripping up the owner's slipper.

Yes, the human life has an extra special gift. It has the ability of conscious *awareness*.

Imagine again for a second that you are the dog, bounding around the house, thinking about being hungry, where the ball is or is that sound of the owner coming back through the door after work? The dog has a constant stream of mind activity that is present to the current situation. It is on a need basis.

The human mind also has this capability. Through the human created perception of time, mankind often spends a lot of time thinking about past or future (something which is not present in the dog and something we will discuss later). But as a human we have another capability, unique to ourselves and that is the ability to be conscious of our self. We are capable of being completely conscious of our thinking and not just 'be the thinking', lost in mental thoughts like the dog.

This the Yogis regard as an incredible gift to all humans as each had the possibility of knowing themselves in their purest form. In this way, life can become aware of itself, its own creation and also itself in others. This is the greatest universal gift available.

You, have been given the greatest gift the Universe has to offer. In fact, to be more precise, *you are* the greatest gift in the Universe.

So here you are a 'perfect gift' from the Universe to itself. So why is it that you find yourself sitting reading a book about self-help?

Well quite simply the gift has *forgotten* what it is.

When we look at a baby or young child, it's often possible to detect a spark of life that exists in them that seems to radiate out to whomever they come in contact with. Their eyes sparkle and appear to be completely at one with life. This is because they are.

When we had just recently come into this world, we were closest to the essential spark of life that we were before the beginning of this being we call 'me'. As youngsters, we still vibrate with the life that is our true essence. We live in the moment and soak up everything that life has to offer, like a wide-eyed sponge. This is the Universe being able to be conscious of itself. The pure essence of life that still exists in the child is capable of seeing its own wondrous *creation* and marvels with loving *joy*.

Then at some certain age humans begin to get absorbed by all of the things that the mind perceives as 'other'. A child may learn to call themselves 'I' or 'me', they then also quickly learn to distinguish things other than themselves. This is how they get mum to realise that they need teddy or wish to get picked up. Time goes on and the child becomes aware of this too. The child may then ask "are we there yet?" or "when will we get there?" The child can now isolate itself as the child that was sad yesterday, scared about tomorrow's dentist and missing its lost blanket. All of a sudden, the human child which was so full of zestful love and joy at being in this moment and feeling at one with everything around has become isolated, vulnerable and plagued by the incessant mind which is now continuously trying to separate its idea of who it is, from everything else.

Through the challenges of adolescence and the difficulties of adulthood this can often intensify until we find that the young child has now become fully immersed in the belief that it is what the mind says it is. It has completely forgotten its true nature, which still exists as an inner 'knowing', but now lies buried under a mountain of mental imagery.

This perception that the mind builds of itself is called the 'Ego' and it is one of the major reasons for the lack of harmony or happiness in humans. It must be mentioned here that the ego is not a personal problem. It is a human trait. Common to all. It is amazingly also an energy source capable of propelling you back to that place where you were full of the spark of life, blissfully happy and one with everything.

So being human is a fairly complex journey. It is not too surprising that with all this happening we may lose sight of our true nature. Forgetting the blissful simple *awareness*, we were when we first lived. Fortunately, it is only 'forgotten' and with some guidance from this book, other guides that will inevitably now come your way and some 'letting go' from you, it will just be a matter of time before that true happiness returns.

Chapter Two

EGO

IT IS QUITE IMPORTANT that we take a bit of time to better know this part of us labelled the 'Ego'. As mentioned previously: It is a key reason for much of our unhappiness and also a big part of the solution to the same.

So, what is this thing the Yogi's call "Ego" which has been written about for thousands of years?

In essence, our ego is *who we think we are*. It is based on ideas such as what we have, what we have done and what we believe other people think of us. It is constantly adding to itself and has been since the very first moment we decided to have a perception of ourselves as 'separate'.

The concepts that it adds to itself are usually compatible with the energy levels of that which already exist. So, for example a teenage girl who does not think she is very pretty may find herself only remembering certain parts of a conversation which involved some dialogue that could have been directed at her being unattractive, even if that was not the intent of what was being said. She may feel as though others are judging her as 'unpretty' or she may avoid mirrors, as her own opinion of her looks are even harsher still.

It is probable that at some point in time during her younger years something happened or was said to her whilst she was still building the picture of 'who she is'. Something that made her believe that she was not pretty enough. It could've been something as simple as mother shouting, "Go and brush your hair, you can't leave the house looking like that, you look awful!" Even a slightly indirect opinion such as this can be enough of a painful shock to her young ideology of who she is, that her mind decides as she looks in the mirror brushing her hair that, "mum is right, I do look awful".

Often an emotion attaches to this mental thought. This may include such feelings as sadness, disappointment or unworthiness etc. It is notable because it may now be the case that this emotion appears each time this thought, or new added unattractive thoughts, arise. It may also work in reverse so that a sad emotion brings up feelings of unworthiness. In this way, an accumulation of emotional pain and thoughts trigger and re-trigger each other; supporting, building and justifying.

So now we skip forward 20 years and a young thirty something woman sits alone at a high school reunion. She had had a few boyfriends/partners over the years since but it never usually lasts long before she starts 'self-sabotaging' the relationship with thoughts of unworthiness, which cause depression and or reactions that to the new man in her life may seem quite unexpected and unjustified. Pretty soon he is giving her less attention and her ego immediately puts this down to her being 'not good enough' for him. "It's always the same thing," she may say, or even worse she will blame the men in her life, "why are men so judgmental and shallow?" Little does she realise that it is just a historical accumulation of thoughts and emotions that keep recreating the same events in her life.

In the ancient beliefs of Yoga these thoughts and emotions that occur and reoccur are called 'Samskaras' they can be described as micro-impressions, almost like negatives on a film or data on a hard-drive. The Yogis also believe that it is these impressions which make up the ego and are the principle cause for what they call 'Karma', the actions and reactions that need to be continually played out in this life time or (they believe) subsequent lives.

In the example above the young lady was plagued by unhappiness about being physically unattractive, but of course there are many other possible scenarios. A middle-aged man dealing with alcohol issues to help him hide pain relating to loss or embarrassment, a teenage bully looking for attention or a shy nervous mother standing back from all the mums at kindergarten trying not to be noticed. Each of the above are having their own egoic response to something that occurred at some time previous.

Is it their fault?

Of course not, how could it be. An ego is not something we need to judge as wrong, it just is.

If we judge our thoughts and emotions as wrong then we just add another emotional layer to them. More wrong-ness to blame yourself for.

No, ego is not wrong, ego is just the unconscious mind making up stories about itself, these thoughts make it continue to be. The human ego is not a personal issue at all. It has momentum passed on from human to human over many thousands of years. It is part of being human. At least until you realise firstly that it exists and secondly that you actually no longer need an ego. Making this admission that your mind made belief of who you are is not who you are, is the 'beginning of the end' of the ego.

Whether you are sleeping in a cardboard box at night on the street reminiscing of a life that you think went so wrong, feeling 'completely alone' whilst sitting eating caviar surrounded by so called rich 'pals' or sitting reading this from a prison cell, it matters only that you recognise that the events that are occurring in your life can be altered. It is as simple as becoming 'aware' of the difference between *what you are* and wh*at your mind tells you* you are.

As you can see: the ego has a simple way of allowing us to believe we are a bunch of accumulated thoughts and opinions. We have become so accustomed to believing what it has to say about ourselves and everything 'else'. As by the flow of karma it continuously 'reinforces' these thoughts, by using thoughts to create *actions* which thereby create *reactions* and *consequences*.

For generations going back to time immemorial humans have replaced the awareness of their true being with the mind based little me or ego that suffers life, instead of being the canvas on which life paints itself. The negative thoughts and self-judgements can be passed down in a similar way to DNA. They are inherent in human nature and are therefore not a personal problem. You could consider the ego as you would the seemingly useless and often problematic appendix. It is something that has grown and adapted and been passed down, inherent in us still, although we have no knowledge of its reason for being present.

So, if this ego thing is not a personal problem then should we be angry, upset or disappointed that we have an ego?

No. Having negative feelings towards the ego will only compound or reinforce it. By adding another layer of negativity towards our thoughts about who we are. This can create self-blame or self-hatred etc.

The ego is not only 'not bad', but a knowledge of its sheer presence can also be seen as being *essential* to learning that which prevents us from being free from karma and seeing ourselves as the 'life of life'.

The ego *can* be dissolved and *awareness* of it is the first step, a step which you have taken already. Distancing yourself from that which you think you are will become easier as you continue to remain aware of how it forms. We will discuss this more later.

However, for now we need to understand more about the mind and its role in forming and consolidating ego.

Chapter Three

MIND

THOUGHTS, MIND AND THE accumulation of such, as ego, are merely ripples in the consciousness of that which we truly are.

If you have ever done any meditation, you may have become aware of the blissful stillness that can sometimes be noticed when the mind is inactive. Like a pond with a still surface, this is the consciousness that you are. If we imagine a small fish now flitting under the surface of the water, you will become aware of the disturbance that occurs to the once still surface of water as ripples radiate outwards. This can be considered as the mind's activity on the surface of our still pond consciousness. As the fish moves away the mind and ripples calm and stillness always returns. It is therefore always possible to return to stillness.

However, as humans we utilise thoughts as an essential part of our daily life. So, we do not need to always have a silent mind. What we need to do is 'not mind what happens'.

What does this mean?

Well it simply means that instead of reacting to the thoughts that arise about particular events, we just allow the events to be. If a thought arises based on previous experiences, knowledge or reactions then it is just that, a simple thought. If we sit in the sun and think it is hot. Then it is just that. We could then use that simple thought to accept the situation or change it if we are feeling uncomfortable.

Free thoughts like this are similarly unproblematic in such a way to using the mind to remember the best route home or to calculate a quick sum when shopping. This is what makes humans capable of doing many things more than other animals and also what makes them equipped to be eventually aware of their true nature as consciousness.

Let us return to the above example, although this time as we are sitting in the sun we get the same thought and instead of allowing it to be a simple *informative thought* we allow our mind to become restless and 'reactive' to the situation. We may suddenly begin to get irritated and react with a shortened temper or aggravated persona which just seconds ago was not even conceivable. We may begin to add fear to the situation and quickly imagine we are getting, not just badly sunburnt, but all kinds of potential future complications such as skin cancer. These thoughts may make us even more agitated or create further negative emotions. This may affect how we react to those around us. Of course, things like sunburn etc. are a possibility but we need only to use our mind to remember that exposure to too much sun is not healthy and then *change the situation*.

In this way, we have used mind as it should be. We were aware of something then we made an assessment based on previous experience and it's now up to us to make a change. The alternative sees us becoming embroiled in a mind-made landslide of negative thoughts and emotions that can affect not just ourselves but those around us. We became a *slave to our mind* and thoughts instead of 'using it' to find a simple solution.

Like riding a wild horse, we find that taking back the reins of the mind gives us, not only control but an easier ride.

As humans, we have the gifted right to use our minds for what we need. Logical thinking, analysing, calculating, remembering etc. What we also often do is allow our mind to jump around (as the Yogis say) like a Monkey. We lose ourselves in its incessant chatter. Losing at the same time the ability to see life in the simple and relatively harmless form that it always takes. Our mind often complicates this moment and as we shall see, the 'now' is always so very simple and perfectly suited for easy living.

With the mind thrashing around ideas based on emotions as in the above example; we start to see how it is, that the ego begins to build itself into that which we think of ourselves. We believe we become the one who reacts badly in situations such as when we are being exposed to too much sun. Remaining free from reaction in this situation would have allowed the ego no opportunity to add or justify its existence. In fact, it would have helped to *dissolve* it, allowing you to use the stillness of a single moment to begin to bring more presence and awareness into the now.

The now is one of the easiest ways to access this stillness of your true self and be able to see the mind activity and emotions as they arise. In this way, you will be becoming aware of the *now* in which all things happen. The now is in essence *this moment, as it always is.* The pure stillness from which all things can be witnessed. It is impartial and also eternal.

When we think about this moment it often gets overlooked because the mind spends a lot of its time thinking about the past or future. In this way, the mind is so preoccupied with events of the past or events 'yet to happen' that it often fails to notice that there is actually only one time and that is now. What happened in the past happened in the *now*, what will happen in the future will be in the *now* also.

Therefore, to help prevent a restless mind, what we really need to do is understand how to recognise this now, access it and remain in it. These actions, which sound very simple, can be an easy way to remove all past and future mental distractions from our lives, such as those built on guilt and fear. What we then start to see is that we do not need to dwell on the past, fear the future or even need to change the future to suit us, to make ourselves happy.

Ego has a lot to do with the creation of this aversion to the present moment. Simply because it gains much of its existence from past/guilt and future/fears etc. The ego ceases to be in the now and this is another very worthwhile reason for harnessing the simple and yet truly transformative power of this moment.

So how do we access the simple *stillness* of the now?

We can use a number of ways of becoming fully present such as breath awareness, inner body awareness, meditation or even simple acceptance of this 'is-ness of now'. What all of these practices do, is to bring you into presence by *stilling the mind*. Breath awareness and body awareness give the mind something else to concentrate on which is happening right here, right now (see appendix A for methods). Both can be as simple as closing the eyes and using the mind to simply watch the breath or attempt to feel the body from within. These can be done in any situation but of course are easier done when surrounding events are calm. However, with regular practice they can be utilised in events that would normally require a high level of mental activity.

Another way of beginning to witness the still presence of the now, in which all things unfold, is to simply *accept all that is*. If you stop applying resistance to what is eventuating, then you will soon begin to see a gap that occurs in this moment, which allows you to feel the freedom of existence without constant mental noise. Acceptance of what is; means having *no resistance* to whatever occurs. This is a very powerful transformative ability and yet is also one of the easiest ways in which to access the now.

Once you have successfully accessed the now, you begin to get a feeling of what it is to be free from not only thought, but emotions and complications of past/future. Subsequently you begin to lose your perception of who you are (your ego) and you start to become aware of your Self as that, which is the silent stillness beyond all that. No different to the now or even life itself.

Many years ago, I sat in a sauna room, alone, eyes closed and meditating on the peace and serenity of the silent stillness in the heated room. Soon enough I was joined by a few other men who entered the room and took up places on the wooden benches around. Most sat quietly, however others chatted normally. Then a group of younger men entered the room and began to chat noisily and laugh out loud. I remained aware of the noise and those around me but my mind accepted all that was happening without judgement and I was able to remain in a joyous blissful state of peace. The noise continued for about ten minutes and then disappeared as most slowly left the room. I decided a short while later that I had had enough of the heat and went out to the changing room. The room was filled with men and as they all moved, on I noticed a man staring at me from the other side of the room. He was a large man seemingly of islander descent, possibly Fijian or Maori. I finished putting on my shoes and stood up to leave and at last he seemed he could no longer contain his curiosity. He loudly asked, "With all of that noise going on in that room, how was it possible that you were able to meditate?" I stopped and looked at the man and simply stated, "If nothing is going on in the mind, then nothing is going on".

Chapter Four

THOUGHTS AND POSITIVE THINKING

THOUGHTS COME AND GO and in the ever-thinking mind they are coming thick and fast. But what are thoughts? Where do they actually come from? How deep do they go? I will not attempt to answer these scientifically and neither do we need to understand them. But if we can stay present and bring some space in after a thought, just a small gap, then you can start to answer these questions and gain a game-changing piece of understanding into why it is we suffer so much.

When we have thoughts, they are just thoughts.

If you stop for a moment and look at a thought after it has arisen, you will start to see what it is and more importantly what it is not.

Thoughts accumulate on top of each other. Sometimes they group together if they bring out the same emotional response in the body. So, jealousy thoughts may bound together or fear etc. Then in the future if another simple similar thought arises in the mind, no matter how briefly, the other thoughts and connected emotion(s) may potentially arise and you can start to become lost in those thoughts or overwhelmed by that emotion. This of course increases the storage for next time.

To break this habit, we need to be aware that these thoughts are just that. They do not hold any real truth. They are mostly just personal opinions and often quite unlike the truth unfolding. Here mindfulness is key to catching these thoughts as they arise so that you do not get lost in the following habituation of further thoughts and emotions.

When mind thinks of something perceived as a 'negative thought' it may cause an emotion; such as imagining the loss of something causing fear. If there is a continued *repetition* of this thought and subsequent emotion it may bring into existence the outcome you feared. This occurs through belief of the initial thought and action based on the emotion felt.

But if you were to stop when you feel this emotion (which could be a trigger for remembering stillness) you may begin to become aware that the emotion and the thought, are not you. By coming through a point of *stillness*, you can reassess the thought, with mind now under your control and see that there is no reaction this time. You can then see the situation as positive and allow the emotion e.g. fear of loss to be removed from yourself. Preventing the belief that this will happen and changing your "own good future" as the Dalai Lama puts it. He points to the fact that the secret to his own happiness is that this/his good future, is in his own two hands. Why would you not wish for that opportunity (by being unhappy and attracting unwanted situations).

He stays positive, thinks positive and attracts positivity.

When we are in a negative state of mind we can perceive naturally occurring situations with a negative outlook. Thus, creating potential suffering when it is not necessary.

For example, if you are suffering from some depression, you may think that the reason people are not calling you back or responding to your messages is because they are ignoring you or suddenly do not like you. However, the reality is often found that after, usually when you are feeling better, you hear from them and find out that they were just too busy to respond or missed your message.

The interpretation of events that you experience in your daily existence can be seen as like a dimensional projection of that state in which your mind resides. If you are feeling a lack of self-confidence then you will often interpret events in such a way that the mind establishes and reinforces a deeper lack of confidence by focusing on those events that it sees as negative or evoking emotions or doubts about situations. Therefore, it is necessary to see the activity of the mind in these events and begin to understand that in the seeing of the mind, we can actually recognise and prove that we are not the mind. We are the *witness* of the mind, established in a place of stillness. The more we reside in this stillness the more we begin to see that when we 'do not mind' what happens, events appear to turn out far more favourably. What is in fact happening is that mind is not being allowed to 'run the show' and interpret events as negative or unfavourable.

The power of positive thinking can bring many good fortunes and seemingly favourable events; however, a time will come when with deepest surrender to your true self you no longer find the need for life to play out in any such way. It *just is* and in this, it is perfect. Right and wrong disappear and all is as it should be. Then a true bliss arises inside. It arises from the fact that you are aware of yourself as consciousness. The Yogis call this "Sat-Chit-Ananda"; meaning *existence-consciousness-bliss.*

Chapter Five

ACCEPTANCE OF WHAT IS / NO RESISTANCE

THERE ARE THREE VERY extremely normal human mind-based functions that occur commonly in most people and which not only strengthen the ego, but subsequently block our ability to be aware of our true blissful nature.

These are Judgement, Attachment and Resistance. To make them a little easier to remember we could call them J.A.R. or some of you may prefer the word RAJ. The key is to finding a simple way to remember these as they will be needed often to start with. They are all of equal importance as keys to unlocking our true nature and finding peace *within* ourselves, *as* ourselves.

The first of these we should look at is resistance, which as we eluded to in the previous chapter can also be described by its opposing action; *acceptance*.

As we have learned the *serenity* that can be found in this moment, is often completely blurred out by the 'noisy mind'. Much of this can usually be attributed to one of the three JAR factors.

Resistance to 'what is', is one of the key factors that can influence your 'state of mind' at any given moment.

A classic example of resisting what is, can be seen in a queue. They say that patience is a virtue and is often a skill learned from previous similar circumstances such as queue standing.

Now let us imagine two people are standing at the end of a very long queue. To even the example up, let us imagine they are both on a day off from work with no other commitments for the remainder of the day.

One is totally at peace with the situation, this person has completely accepted the fact that the queue is long and that it is going to take some time before they get to do what they are lining up for. They have accepted the situation and their mind is offering no resistance. By simply allowing this event to be, they are now at one with this moment. They are at peace, possibly smiling and finding joy in what would seem like an unenjoyable situation.

Standing one place in front of them (so actually closer to the goal) is another person whose mind is full of objection to the fact that the queue is so long and that they will have to wait. They cannot accept that this is something that should be happening to them and therefore they are completely at odds with the present moment. They are in a total state of *inner resistance* against the events of the now. Their mind is now likely coming up with a whole variety of problems, both past, present and future, such as reasons why they were late and ended up so far back in the queue (maybe even blaming others for this) or concerning over losing time on their day off. They are probably experiencing a whole range of emotions such as anger, fear, resentment and general unhappiness.

Two people, same queue.

Resistance to what is in any situation is not only futile but as we shall see, it actually draws more negativity into an event. How many times has a workman got upset with a particular job before reacting angrily and then hitting their thumb with a hammer, or a young child kicks an object out of frustration, stubbing their toe and getting more upset?

This sort of resistance can be clearly seen in 'road rage' situations where often one or more drivers of vehicles fail to accept a situation on the road and this inner resistance to what is begins to grow to a stage where it can often lead from slight frustration to intensified anger and physical violence.

There will be many times in our daily lives in which we offer some resistance to what is. If it is a situation that we cannot change or leave then it will not be long before frustration and other negative emotions begin to arise. We do not always have to accept situations if they are unsuitable and we have an option of changing them. In essence, we always usually have a choice.

If the person standing frustrated in the queue suddenly decides that they will come back another day then the situation will likely ease, however they may take it with them as unhappy past and be angry that they never got to do what they intended to. If we look closely we will see this is resistance again.

The person sitting in the sun from our earlier example may decide to get up and move to the shade. This is acceptance also. If they do have no option but to stay in the sun like a cricket player at an important match then they should take necessary sun-protection precautions and then accept that this is enough. Resistance would cause their mind to not only be unhappy but also to lose focus on what they are hoping to achieve from the activity.

Chapter Six

ATTACHMENT / DESIRES

WHEN, PROBABLY AS A small child, we first began to identify ourselves as separate from all other things, we began to think along the lines of I, me and mine. Pretty soon we began to utilise this to feel individuality and ownership for example 'I' am tired or please feed 'me' or that ball is 'mine'. So, you can see how we begin to become *attached* to objects very quickly. A child that has a favourite blanket, will say, "the blanket is mine" and all you would need to do is try and convince the child to give you the blanket to realise that this sense of 'mine' is an incredibly strong bond.

But what makes it such a powerful bond?

What the child has done by instilling the blanket with a sense of mine, is to actually make the blanket a part of their 'self'. They have applied so much dependence and importance into the object that it has now become part of who they believe themselves to be, "I am 'so and so' and this is my blanket, it is 'mine' and not yours."

When you try and remove this object from the child, the sadness and tears that come are from attachment, not only to the object but also to the feeling of loss of a part of self. Thoughts may arise such as "what will I be without my blanket?", "I need it", "if I do not have a blanket and someone else does then I am less than they?".

This simple example of a child's blanket can then be expanded to encompass almost everything that is believed to be acquired by a person as they grow up and begin to accumulate things. But it is not just objects that we put into our accumulated belief of who we are. Friends, appearance/looks, education, job, fitness/strength all fall into this basket of 'me'.

These things are of course all perfectly fine in the life of a person, as is the warm and comforting blanket of a child, but what we now have is an object with a subject. Something that contributes to 'me' and more importantly an attachment that, if it were to be lost, would cause suffering. If we look at most of the suffering that occurs in a human life it can be attributed to an attachment such as this. What we have done is started to believe that our happiness depends on this particular circumstance or object to which we are attached.

There are obvious instances of this: an attachment to a partner whose leaving causes heartache, or to the ability to do things with a young body which will cause frustration as old age arrives or even to a certain lifestyle only available whilst earning large sums of money etc. But also, there are many subtle attachments and these can often be the ones that fill the day with unhappiness and dissatisfaction. These could be as simple as somebody not answering your call when you phone them or a 'good time' coming to an end.

As you can begin to see, a major problem with attachments and the *suffering* they cause is due to the notion of unfavourable events unfolding in time.

What all of these attachments hold can be linked to what we have previously discussed and will discuss further regarding no judgement, no resistance and the incessant need for the mind to habituate itself in past or future. The mind loves to believe that it deserves certain 'outcomes' and of course if those outcomes are not exactly as the mind so wishes, then it is automatically perceived as unfavourable and often a trusted attachment is 'mercilessly torn apart by life'.

Or at least that's what the mind thinks.

What in actual fact has happened is that life is taking its normal turn of natural events in which all form is forever changing, but due to an attachment of how it should be, the mind now feels hard done by.

It is indeed the case that if we allow things to be, without fear of certain outcomes, then events unfold in a way that seem incredibly favourable. What is in fact happening is that we are no longer placing any *attachment* (part of our self) onto a specific required outcome.

This could be your first car that eventually needs to be scrapped or finishing up the 'best party ever'. We can replace attachment to these with enjoyment of them whilst they last. This is ok. To do so we just need to remember they are not what makes us who we are and that *no-thing* lasts forever. As the wise old saying says, "This too will pass". This is something that can be remembered and applied often during your day. It applies not just to bad times that you wish would pass (acceptance) but also to good times that you hope will never end. In both cases it allows you to separate from attachment and find acceptance or enjoyment.

Then we begin to realise that the happiness and joy we thought were due to that particular object or circumstance was actually not the case at all. The *joy*, which is our *true nature*, was flowing out of us into the situation and not the other way around. This joy can never be lost and although it can be forgotten, it can also always naturally be remembered.

Staying firmly in the knowledge that all things (including events and situations) are impermanent will help to surpass the suffering caused by attachments. It will also help you to realise that within you is something permanent that is aware of this.

Only something permanent could notice the impermanence in all other things.

Chapter Seven

JUDGEMENT

JUDGEMENT IS STRONGLY LINKED to resistance and attachment. If we do not resist life we will find ourselves being less judgemental and similarly if we have no attachments to objects or outcomes we find the same.

It is however something that we need to look at specifically also, as judgement comes in many forms and is another one of the minds tools for creating separation and therefore another reinforcement of ego and a false sense of self.

We have spoken quite a bit about judging events as favourable and unfavourable etc. Let us now turn our attention to understanding how we also *judge* ourselves and others.

A mind which believes itself to be separate, enjoys nothing better than judging. As we saw in the previous example of the young girl who believed herself to be unattractive, she would possibly spend much of her life, including many of her interactions with others and her own personal thoughtful times, judging herself as so. Her mind would constantly reinforce the ego by (who she thinks she is) with negative thoughts of not being good enough.

Judging one's self harshly with negative thoughts like this will not only reinforce the ego and feelings of separation but it will attract further such situations as we have discussed. The unfavourable events are strangely enough, both desired by the mind (to further confirm its own ideas of itself), but also complained about by the mind as judging others as causing us to feel unattractive. Mind will also try and judge us as inferior to others by being less attractive to others.

As you can see, when we judge ourselves we bring about a certain amount of misery, separateness and difference from others and similar situations and occurrences which cause further suffering.

Judging others also has the same repercussions.

If we were to take the example of two brothers, one of which thought his parents favoured his sibling. Then we would often see that in this situation the judgement from the seemingly less favoured brother would often create the circumstances in which he believes himself to be.

He may start off simply by reacting unfavourably as a young child to the fact that his brother got the red truck and he the blue. Judging his parents for their inaptitude at choosing good presents or his brother for being the favoured child. Maybe he decides to throw his truck down out of disgust or try and grab his brothers truck. How will this affect his relationship with his brother or his parents?

Could it be that his reactions begin to create some small favour towards his brother rather than himself? If it does, will it not continue to reinforce his beliefs and judgements?

In saying that he deserves his truck to be red, he has judged himself to be *right* and his parents *wrong* as well as favouring his brother. He has also judged his brother, not only as being favoured, but also as not being deserving of a red truck.

In this way we can see that mind not only tries to reinforce separateness by judgement of others as working against the 'me', but also by making the me right and the others wrong. This becomes very obvious in an 'egotistical' person who always believes themselves to be right and others wrong. They bring others down in their own mind or the mind of others to elevate their own perceived status.

As you can begin to see, there are many ways in which the mind uses judgement to its self-creating benefit.

But what are these judgements and how much power do they really have?

Judgements are mind made thoughts based on personalised opinions of what we believe to be right or wrong. It is as simple as that.

Are they factual in any way? To answer this simply, how can they be? They are just personalised opinions.

In this way we can see that if someone judges you as this or that, it does not automatically mean that is what you are. In fact, if we judge their opinion as more important than ours or someone else's, is that not just *another* judgemental thought?

If we look at what creates our own judgements, these personalised opinions have been formed by your mind due to its own interpretation of events that it perceived during your life time. When we look at judgements like this, we start to see that they have no real validity and really hold as little substance as would a recollected interpretation of a dream.

Chapter Eight

BREAKING FREE FROM JUDGING, RESISTING AND ATTACHING

A S WE CAN SEE from the previous few chapters there are vast amounts of suffering created by the human mind as it struggles to reinforce its own believed existence as separate to everything else by *judgement, resistance* and *attachment.*

To break free from these, we need to start to firstly remember that these are just indeed human traits. Even the great sages of the past such as Buddha and Jesus etc. were all at some point in their existence sufferers of one or all of these attributes.

They are both natural and universally common, so they must not be taken personally. To do so would just further compound the suffering. So, let us just take it that, as humans, we all have them at some stage just like wisdom teeth or a common cold.

In allowing them to be, we start to distance our self from them, even if just a little. We put some space between ourselves and the thoughts that create them. Because in essence that is all they are, just thoughts.

Are we our thoughts? No. We are the watcher of the thoughts.

With this knowledge, we can now begin to 'notice' and not 'be' the thoughts. As we become more and more accustomed to noticing these thoughts of judgement, resistance or attachment as they arise, the more we become capable of seeing them as just thoughts. They have *no power over us except for when we believe in them.*

How do we stop 'believing' in them?

We stay completely present as the *is-ness* that remains beyond thoughts. We harbour our attention in the place of witnessing and from here we see the thoughts as merely this. This way, the thoughts do not take on any extra importance or power. As we have already mentioned, the human mind has been barrelling down the highway of self-developing thoughts such as judgements and attachments for thousands of years and it has become part of who we are. We must therefore be patient and accepting, as slowly over time the mind begins to lose its *momentum.* Mind itself, will need to become accustomed to the new change as would a person moving to live in another country.

Gradually as we become more and more 'aware' of the mind, its thought processes and habitual wants, we begin to unravel its needs and expose it for that what it is, just an accumulation of random, meaningless and uncontrolled thoughts.

Where does that leave us?

We now sit as the witness to all this. At peace with the mind. Gradually utilising our, now controllable thoughts more and more just for that which we need in this moment.

In this state, which will grow more and more as we stay in it, we begin to not only prevent that which causes us suffering but we enable ourselves to be at one with life as it unfolds and this in itself begins to bring forth joy from ourselves into this moment and the events that you perceive in your life. This is the beginning of *breaking free*.

Chapter Nine

ACCEPTANCE OF SUFFERING

THE DALAI LAMA POINTS to the fact that 'suffering is human, not personal'. If we catch a cold or flu, we rarely take it personally. It is common to humans and it's the same for *mental* suffering. It is normal. If we take suffering personally, then we add personal negative emotions such as anger or self-hatred on top of what already exists as the perceived original suffering.

Suffering is therefore something that should be accepted, allowed to exist. You should accept that it is something very common to most, if not all, humans at some time and do not take it personally.

As we have seen above, we often associate suffering with our inability to *accept* the *is-ness* of this moment. This often implies that we believe life to be giving us a 'raw deal' or to be treating us unfairly. This implies we have no say in our own happiness, which we have seen is not the case, so for now ask yourself this simple question…

How did you get to this moment of your life right now?

By making millions of small choices throughout your life, the events naturally led to this point.

You are here because of everything you ever did!

In every situation, we always have a choice. Even if we were hog-tied in a dungeon we still have a choice to accept this or not.

So, every choice you ever made got you to this point.

This knowledge is a very powerful tool to helping to accept 'that what is', which cannot be otherwise. Because even if you are suffering, it was a part of you that chose to be here, to endure this suffering to reveal your true self and all that you are. The universe did not just afflict you with this suffering, you chose it and as you shall see, you chose it for a reason.

This is true acceptance, not just the acceptance of what is but acceptance of any suffering caused by denial of what is.

There is always so much to be learned from suffering, once accepted. Acceptance of your choices stops regrets, it accepts the now as your will; allowing any suffering to be surrendered and therefore transformed into the lesson it brings. This is often awareness. By accepting suffering, you often become more deeply aware of that which suffers in you, but also that which *witnesses* the suffering, that which remains partial, your *true self.*

There is also true power and limitless energy hidden within suffering and released by acceptance of such. When we suffer, we store this power within the ego as trapped emotion, as we have mentioned before it can accumulate and attract similar such energies. But just as a person stores firewood for the long cold winter when it is most needed, the suffering when 'burned' from our self by the ignition of the light of self-awareness, fuels the fire that we need, to be propelled into a state of *freedom*.

What is needed to prevent further suffering and burn up existing stores is to *shine the light of awareness* onto it. When you feel something that makes you suffer or are in the midst of suffering, pause when acceptable, even if you have to find a bit of space alone or close your eyes and simply reflect on the suffering. At first you will possibly feel the same pain, but then as you stay with this, you may begin to notice that you and the pain are separate. You may enquire, what is the pain? Is it just a thought? Who is feeling it? The more you stay present the more you will begin to see that you and the sufferer, or the notion of suffering, are not one and the same. You are safely distanced. Like a young child who looks away from the TV in a scary movie to remember that it is not real.

A great deal of inner power can be hidden in our previous suffering so we should not judge suffering as bad. Doing so only personalises it. Once we remove this judgement we will start to see that it has a part to play, a very important part, in helping us become who we are meant to be. In helping us to be not only free from any and all suffering but to be one with the peace and joy that comes with that knowing.

We only need to look as far as the Dalai Lama, Buddha, Jesus and many other modern-day people who have found true peace and happiness within themselves, to see that they all suffered. I am sure that if you could ask them if suffering was a necessary part of the journey into becoming who they are, they would all agree it had some important part to play.

Acceptance of suffering is not something that has to continue forever. Once you realise that you no longer have to stop suffering to be free, then it has played its part. Freedom from this suffering is what the Buddhists call "Nirvana".

Chapter Ten

THE NOW –
BEING PRESENT

A S YOU CAN SEE there are many ways to free ourselves from the suffering, that comes in so many forms in human existence, suffering such as depression, anxiety, fear etc.

There is one common factor to all of these techniques that also is the key itself to freedom, unbound joy and peace. Owning to this common factor are many names such as presence, is-ness/what is or simply 'the now'.

All of the methods available for accessing freedom utilise the now in some way or another. The now itself is also the place where freedom only exists. There cannot be any suffering in the now. As soon as the now or present awareness is brought to suffering, *it ceases to be*.

As was aforementioned, the now is a place wherein time and a personal me cease to exist. Losing time means losing the suffering of past events and any suffering being caused by worrisome thoughts of future events also.

Removing the personal 'me' means losing ego and all of the suffering of accumulated thoughts stored under the heading 'who I think I am'.

As we enter the now, through one of the techniques given in this book, we start to see that time no longer exists and neither does the 'me'. This is due to the fact that the deep surrender that occurs to this moment when we enter the now, allows us to go beyond the uncontrolled mind and mental activity that creates these *delusions*.

Time is a human creation and is not relevant to animals or trees. A dog may sense that its belly is empty and feel hungry around a certain time each day which makes it look for food but this is just a natural response, common to most animals and essential for life. Humans on the other hand look at a clock saying 11am and think 'it's really too late for breakfast, I'd better get some early lunch'.

Humans created the entire concept of time, they measure it and also run their lives around it. Time is of course something created out of necessity as we have evolved and become more advanced. It helps us to meet each other or catch planes etc. So, time in itself is not bad. But when we begin to attach time to the image we have of who we are, it begins to create suffering. 'I am not as fit as I used to be', 'She doesn't love me anymore', 'I think they will probably ask me to leave the team'. All of these are examples of us projected 'out of the now' to describe who we are, were or will be, yet none of which can exist in the now.

In this moment *we are as we are*. We lose all judgements of what happened in the past and all fears of what will be in the future. We simply are, here and now.

This freedom from past or future once witnessed even for the briefest moments, begins to naturally justify itself as the acceptance of not being able to change the past and not being able to predict the future. In reality whatever we think of the future, it will not play out as we expect. Acceptance of these two factors are no different to complete surrender to the now.

Being present in the now (this moment) also enables us to go, not only beyond the suffering caused by time, but also the suffering caused by all other facets of the suffering 'me'.

In the now we begin to notice that there is not only 'no time' but strangely enough we find it difficult to locate what it is that we actually call 'me'. As we stay present in the moment, *just being*, we find there is no actual location of me. There may be the odd thought floating across like a cloud in the sky but when it passes and our presence remains, the thing we once thought of as 'who we are' is suddenly known to be not present. Like a teacher doing a roll call, the naughtiest child no longer responds 'yes Miss, here I am'.

Instead there is pure emptiness. No more self-judgement. No more sadness or anger, all is gone. All of the thoughts of who you think you are have simply vanished. Free from any suffering caused by desires or aversion, no longer trapped in a world ruled by uncontrollable outcomes. Everything in the now is simply as it is and better still, completely *as it should be*. It cannot be any other way.

As the thoughts of yourself as a little 'me' with all of its attachments disappear, they leave behind a seeming vacuum of space which naturally pulls in a much subtler awareness. One which has no suffering, no attachments, no need for past or future, no judgements of good or bad, no desires or aversions, no fear, no depression...

This is your true self. It is who you are, not who you think you are.

Chapter Eleven

BEING TRUE TO YOURSELF BY BEING YOUR TRUE SELF

WHEN YOU FIRST GET a glimpse of who you truly are, your true self, it is a moment you will not simply forget. In a single moment all that you believed yourself to be is erased. What remains is a knowing that you are free from all that ever caused you any suffering. You are fully present in the one and only perfect moment of now. You are faultless, flawless and beyond compare. There is no longer a self that can be affected by thoughts, just a self that *witnesses all*.

This 'I' that remains as your true self, is no longer separate from events or people. It doesn't see itself as 'me and them' or as a victim of time and events unfolding. It blends with all that is and any of the mental boundaries that once caused the illusion of separateness simply disappear again.

In this way you begin to see life as you did many years ago. As a young child possibly, who knew only joy and oneness with life. This is not only our true self but our true nature. It is how we came into the world. Before we became disillusioned by thoughts of separateness and a false belief of who we are.

As you return to being your *true self* you will begin to see that the harshness of life caused by perceived separation disappears and life simply becomes *that* in which you can once again be as joyous and care-free as a young child.

You become as a witness to the life unfolding in front of your eyes. You become the life of life itself. Creation witnessing its own creation.

Then as you begin each day, instead of expectancy or dread, you start the day with zero and with the belief that by the end of the day you will also have zero. This does not mean that you will never gain anything in your life. You will just not attach to or lose anything. This brings great peace.

The key to being more and more present in this state is by actually just being more and more in this state.

'Practice makes progress!' as my son always says.

As you spend time in the knowing, you will *become* the knowing. As you find this state over and over during moments of quietude, you will later be able to access this peace during moments of unrest.

Just being, as your true self, will become something you love. It will bring you greater joy than anything you have experienced or can ever experience. It is the source of true joy and happiness, bliss.

Chapter Twelve

MIND/EGO PUTS UP A FIGHT

A S WE PROGRESS ALONG the journey of self-realisation, there may come a time when the ego-mind, which is the delusion of self, begins to resist destruction. Almost like a snake that has been cut. It appears for a brief while to fight more ferociously, as if feeling its own *imminent* demise.

The mind may seemingly find another gear and race away with all manner of thoughts. Some of which may seem like incessant, negative thoughts that re-occur and reinforce themselves. Although often very unpleasant, this process which can be likened to the phenomenon 'Anxiety', is a natural reaction and often necessary in the journey of self-discovery. It therefore needs not to be worried about, as this will again only add further negativity to the situation.

It must be remembered that if there is any power it is not with the mind, it has no power of its own. You however as your true self are already the life of life.

One possible way to overcome these mental attacks is to remember to pause whenever the negativity is felt (usually as emotion caused by thought) and ask yourself 'Who is suffering this?'. Through persistent self-enquiry you will eventually find that 'no-one' is actually suffering and that the thoughts are suffering themselves. When you reach this stage, you can also look more deeply and ask 'who am I that knows this?'. The practice of 'self-enquiry' is a very powerful tool and much is written about this technique.

Many of the other techniques discussed in this book will be beneficial in passing though this stage. Being present is again key.

Sometimes however it may just occur that it is not possible, as the anxiety of an actively fighting ego-mind can prevent easy access to the now.

There are however other things that you can do if you cannot find the time, space or gaps between incessant thoughts to meditate. Often, we find that doing something that makes us happy can help, but this may not always suffice. In times when suffering feels very oppressive and the mind feels unbeatable, when tears coarse down your cheek from depression or fears twist your gut with sickness from anxiety, then stop all that you are doing and do something selfless. Write a note of kindness to someone, let them know you care, make someone smile, include someone who looks alone, do something for someone without them knowing. Selfless means 'no self' is involved and when you are there, then you are free from the suffering that the mind made self can experience.

We see from these actions that although doing something that makes ourself happy is helpful, doing something that makes another happy instantly creates true lasting happiness in return to ourselves. Actions such as this can help to *complete the journey* and finish the complete eradication of ego.

This is often why people who are called 'ego-less' are often steeped in selfless service such as was Mother Theresa. Their ego has simply left them completely. They find no better joy in their hearts than giving to others.

When we give to another we not only make their existence happier or easier, but we also share the love and joy that is in ourselves. We can lighten up their dark times.

Finding the light in ourselves and sharing it with others is often revered as a human's greatest potential. There is no experience more rewarding.

Chapter Thirteen

REST IN PEACE

AS YOU BEGIN TO find your true self and the love that you are and shine this light for others you will begin to notice also that the things you share and enjoy will be returned to you. You may have already begun to notice this *karmic action* and the results it can bring. Love, joy, happiness, feeling welcomed, these and many more, in fact all human emotions, can be returned back to yourself by life as you project them out to others.

In this way, *life looks after life*.

Let it be.

With this truth in your heart, with this knowing in your very being, you can now apply this with some of the other practices and understandings that you will acquire as your journey continues, to help you to come to know yourself as that *life* itself.

Accept what life has to offer always. If you can, enjoy what life has to offer and from time to time allow that enjoyment to coarse through your veins with wild freedom and creativity in the form of enthusiasm. Eckhart Tolle, a wonderful spiritual teacher, points to this by saying that we should always try to be in a state of acceptance, enjoyment or enthusiasm. Anything else and we are resisting life. This will always be futile.

Relax and allow life to be as it is and always have the mindset; *I am that I am.* This will remove all judgement and resistance from your life.

Do not attach yourself to any outcome or need. If you have partners, friends or other relationships that is fine, but 'allow them to be' also, do not require or depend on anything from them. This will remove attachments and allow them to be beautiful relationships firmly based in truth, love and respect of each other's perfection as the 'I am'.

Life itself...

One with all...

This is 'true love'. It is what is meant when someone greets you with the word 'Namaste'. A recognition of true selves as one.

In this 'I am-ness' you can learn to relax and not need to be perfect. *Mind* will cast doubt by throwing up accusations that you are not as good as you should be. This is all just illusory. Your true self is beyond perfection. It needs not try to be anything, it just is. Be that, remove judgement.

Rest in the place of beingness more and more. As you do you will begin to find that it brings you a feeling of great love. As you remain in it more often, your love for it will continue to grow. Eventually you will begin to feel that the love you have for it, is the love you are and the love it is also. A *sacred trinity* in which the knower, the knowing and the known become one. This is your true self.

Relax and live in this love. *Love* and do whatever you wish to. For out of this love, only *true action* can occur. This will align your actions completely with the natural play of life. Within these true actions, suffering for you and others cannot exist.

As you become aware of yourself as this human being (not a human doing) you will find that the peace that you are makes the voice and attractions of the mind become insignificant. As it stands, any thoughts that fade in interest in such a way, cease to become a reality in your consciousness and therefore cease to exist in your life.

This will remove all that makes suffering in your life.

All that is required is for you to find your 'is-ness' and dwell in it.

It is as simple as that. The rest will simply follow, just witness and 'be life' from this place.

If you have walked through a graveyard you may have noticed that written on certain gravestones are the words Rest In Peace (or R.I.P.). It is often written or stated as a prayer that the person should find peace in the 'afterlife.'

Why should it be that we need to die in order to find peace?

Your chance to rest in peace is here, now. Seize it. Be it.

It is your true self and it has a life full of pure joy ahead.

Epilogue

A DAY IN THE LIFE
OF A SEER

EYES FLITTER AND OPEN. The room comes into view. Mind, which was possibly just dreaming moments ago, falls still. An awareness of senses begins to form. The brightness of the sunshine through the windows, the sounds of early morning birds outside, the smell of coffee or toast. All are witnessed but without reaction. They are appreciated for the beauty but not judged as this or that, good or bad.

A feeling of gratitude for this life and this day burst from the heart.

Someone from the family, maybe a child or partner, comes in the room, you feel the same joy burst from your heart but it has no attachment, a oneness is felt, a connection, a knowing that something in you is recognising something in them as itself and vice versa.

Time and events naturally pass. You finish your breakfast and ready for work. There is no need to rush, all is as it should be.

Driving to work you hit a traffic jam stretching for miles. You smile and relax back into the seat. All is as it should be. There is a knowing that you will arrive at work exactly when you mean to and not a moment later.

You turn to look at the driver next to you and although they look agitated you do not judge them for this, you simply smile politely and as you do they seem to breathe a little easier, calm a little more and slowly relax back into their chair also.

As you relax and hold no thoughts of being late, you see the traffic clear and once again you are on your way.

Upon reaching work you have a spring in your step for whatever lays ahead and little events happen like the elevator being open just enough time to hop in and a colleague offering to make you a coffee. You see the beauty in the events and feel appreciative but you do not cling to the events as necessities for happiness. It appears as though your joy is making the event and not the other way around.

The remainder of the day plays out with similar effect. Witnessed and loved for all that it contains. Any harshness of life is simply melted away by the no judgement, no attachment or no resistance. As if completely awake in a dream. The conscious awareness that remains sees life only from the states of complete acceptance, enjoyment or enthusiasm.

You are simply in the world, but not of the world.

As the eyes begin to shut at the end of the day again the self feels gratitude for all that was. Aware that it ends the day fully enriched and yet with the same nothingness that it began the day with.

Sleep descends and the blissful seamless state of consciousness continues.

Appendix A

BODY AWARENESS

USING BODY AWARENESS IS a particularly useful tool in the journey. It can help to allow you to feel present in all situations. With a little practice it can be utilised even in challenging situations to bring you back to peace and stop you from getting lost in mental thought and the ensuing suffering.

In body awareness we allow our focussed attention to be directed inwards to an area of the body, where we safely harness our mind, keeping it from drifting until it no longer feels any need to drift.

It is a simple technique that works so well and in so many situations because the body is with us always and all we need to do is draw our attention within.

To give a small example of body awareness we need simply close our eyes and focus our attention on the palms of our hands. You may become aware of a tingling sensation or some heat in this area. Keep your attention focussed on this area and once you begin to feel this connection, slowly move your hand and follow this sensation as it moves.

Then hold your hand still. Feel the knowing that although your eyes are still shut and you cannot 'see' where your hand is, you still know exactly where it is.

Now take this attention and focus it on your heart centre. Feel the peace that radiates from this area as you hold your attention here. Then gradually move the attention to other areas of the body, sensing any changes as you go.

What you will begin to notice is that as your mind remains fully focussed on the inner sensation of body awareness it loses its need to search outside for external stimulation. Feeling yourself becoming more present.

With attention focussed as such the mind will actually begin to feel like it has the ability to rest.

As you practice this ability you will be able to utilise body awareness to bring yourself into presence. This can be particularly useful in situations in which some people find the mind is quick to assess, judge or add mental commentary. This could be, for example, challenging situations in which you feel stressed or emotional.

It can also be used if you have difficulties talking to people. Ego-mind will often give *imaginary status* to others in an attempt to keep them as something completely different to ourselves. We may see them as lower or higher in status than ourselves and this creates judgement of them and ourselves during conversation. By placing a small amount of your attention into the body, it can centre you, keeping you fully present, allowing the remainder of your attention to be focussed on the conversation but not to get carried away by mental activity, not to be judgemental.

Body awareness can be used before meditation also. The practice can be extended to encompass all areas of the body. Holding awareness in the hands at first or the heart and then travelling the body keeping attention and feeling that part of the body relax as the light of awareness fills it.

BREATH
AWARENESS

B REATH AWARENESS OR 'PRANAYAMA' as it
is called in Yoga is another excellent way of calming
the mind and bringing peace and presence into being.
Again, it is particularly useful in situations that may be
emotionally challenging or practicing prior to meditation
to assist in achieving awareness of true self.

There are many types of breathing techniques, especially
in Pranayama practices, all of which have the capability of
producing positive benefits.

However, to bring our awareness into presence and
peace into our minds we need only practice the simpler
techniques. In this way, as with the other techniques
listed here, we can practice and apply the practice easily
and often.

To begin with, find a comfortable position, once again
it need not be sitting upright, laying down is fine also.
A quiet place may help initially to keep your focus internal.

Close your eyes and slowly become aware of your breathing. As much as possible, do not attempt to control the breath, this can often be a challenge but keep practicing.

Instead, allow the body to breathe as it was before you brought your attention to it. Remembering that the body does not need the mind to control the breathing, it has done it since the moment you were born, even throughout all of your sleep. As the muscle of heart beats in the body so does the muscle of the diaphragm activate the lungs pulling air in and expelling. It is completely natural. Allow it simply to be.

With your awareness remaining on the breath, just 'watch' the breathing flow in and out. By watching we do not mean with the eyes but with our witnessing attention. We need just be aware of the inhalation and exhalation as they pass in and out through either the nose or mouth.

You may be aware of a sound or a feeling/sensation as the breath moves through, just let this be. This can help maintain the awareness.

Simply continue to watch the breathing, keeping your attention focussed purely on this. Allowing yourself to be fully present and mindful.

This technique, similarly to the body awareness, gives you another possible useful technique to employ when needed to help return the awareness to a peaceful state by utilising something that is always present.

Another example of utilising breath awareness in times of stress is simply taking a few conscious deep breaths. Some scientists believe that physiologically it can also help to relax the body system by increasing Oxygen to the brain and lowering blood pressure etc.

Simple breathing techniques like this can be once again practiced and utilised whenever and wherever necessary and take very little time at all.

MEDITATION

ONE OF THE KEY parts to a meditation is the time taken beforehand to make sure you will be comfortable and (in the beginning) as uninterrupted as possible. You pose and location need not be cross legged on a hilltop in the Himalayas for a successful meditative experience. Make sure you are comfortable in whatever position you take, if you wish to lay down, that is fine. If you can be in a place where you will not be interrupted that is great. If not, you can still meditate. Meditation is about allowing the awareness to come away from the senses and the mind. Turn off phones, put a sign up on the door. Remember the meditation you need is the one you will get so if you are interrupted and have to stop, that is ok also. It just means at this point your awareness is needed elsewhere.

In your comfortable position take a few moments to notice how you feel and your mental activity. It is often a good idea to see the before and after to be aware of differences.

Take a few deep breaths and sigh them out. If you wish you can use one of the body or breath awareness practices to quieten the mind or relax the body.

Allow your mind to just be. Do not spend more energy or effort on trying to calm the mind if it is active. Instead just allow it to do its own thing and pay no attention to it. Treat the mind as you may a naughty child or animal that thrives on attention, the less attention you give the more likely it will cease the behaviour. The thoughts are merely clouds drifting across the sky of your awareness, let them drift.

Focus your attention instead at your heart centre. Do not try to imagine anything there. Just allow your awareness to reside in that area, effortlessly.

If you find yourself distracted by the thoughts of the mind and drifting with the mental chatter, if you find yourself as a 'cloud', then just accept this and return to the heart centre, return to being the unchanging 'sky' beyond all clouds.

Focussing your awareness on the heart centre. Allowing thoughts to come and go. This is all that is needed. Stay with this as long as you feel necessary. The more you do this meditation, the more you will be discovered.

Eventually, as you progress with this practice, a time will come when you will be able to take the knowing, peace and mindfulness into the remainder of the day. As they say, the meditator may leave the meditation, but the meditation will not leave the meditator.

STILLNESS
PRACTICE

WATCHING A STAR ON a slightly cloudy night is the perfect way to understand the meaning of focusing and re-focusing on the stillness of mind which will always bring you peace. With your eyes focused on a star, use the time when it is fully visible to stay fully present. This represents what you can achieve within your mind during thoughtless focus on stillness. Then as clouds approach and cover over your star, blocking its view, this represents you becoming lost in thought. The cloud (the thoughts) pass slowly or quickly blocking your ability to see that peace. Once they clear though, the star once again appears and you can re-focus on it once more. Try this exercise if you get a suitable sky at night. It should only take a few minutes but can be so very valuable in understanding how to allow thoughts to pass 'as clouds' pass across the sky, always returning to focus on the stillness behind thoughts.

Book Two

CENTERING IN
YOUR TRUE SELF

Introduction

BREAKING FREE
– MY PERSONAL
STORY

W HEN I WAS IN my mid-forties, I had a life that
would have been the envy of many.

I had a beautiful wife and young family, my own busi-
ness which could be regarded as quite profitable, good
friends and health, a nice house, car and all that a person
could really want. I was happy, content and lived a very
peaceful life, with plenty of time for myself and holidays
around beautiful destinations. Others would deem me
'successful', the lucky friend who 'had it all'.

Then for no apparent reason, I began to suffer from
severe anxiety and depression. It came on with such a
rapid intensity that within no time it had completely
engulfed the life that I lead. It affected every part of the
world I knew. My relationships with both family, friends

and strangers. My work life. I found myself at times almost incapable of facing even those who were closest to me through sheer humiliation. I would spend whole days in bed almost unable to move with inescapable sadness. Alone in my room, this was my safe place. Anxiety, fear and mistrust plagued my life outside of this room and the world quickly went from a place of beauty to an endless environment of horrifying dread.

During sleep, which for a time at the beginning felt like my only escape, I eventually became plagued with intense life-like nightmares.

Life quickly became unrecognisable and completely unbearable. The thought of escaping this life crossed my mind many times.

Although I had many people in my life who offered an incredible amount of support and some of whom helped me to literally make it through each day, it still felt that somewhere deep inside I had to overcome this from within my own self, by myself, medication free, using my own mind to find a 'way out'.

After years of battling through various stages of depression and then severe anxiety; after trying all that I could to find a way out, I began to mentally lose hope. Hope had gotten me through all of this but with no end in sight and different feelings, thoughts and emotions plaguing me consistently even when others had since stopped, I began to give up ever believing that I would once again look at life as anything other than 'hell on earth'.

One morning I got up and felt so incredibly depressed that life no longer had anything left for me. I was standing in the bathroom, head down as usual, too embarrassed to even face myself in the mirror, tears welling in my eyes.

After some time of just staring looking down at the sink, something compelled me to look at myself. As I stared at my rather hopeless and pitiful looking reflection, a thought crossed my mind; what was it that kept me trapped in this misery?

Was it not my thoughts?

This resonated with me, so as I stood staring, I enquired further, almost feeling separate from my thoughts a little; If it was my thoughts that were making me so unhappy, then how were the efforts of all my thoughts going to free me from this suffering?*

At this instant moment I had a sudden realisation that *my mind* was the reason I was trapped in my own misery and that it could never actually help me to be free. In fact, it was almost as if it needed me to remain in this unawareness so that a part of it could continue to exist.

It was at this point that even though I could still feel the emotions of extreme depression and tight-chested anxiety within me, I no longer felt the want to fight it and as if *waving a white flag of truce*, I just stopped trying to be anything other than what I am.

My breathing seemed to suddenly relax and deepen incredibly as if a giant weight had been lifted from my chest.

The reflection in the mirror stared back but for the first time in my life I no longer saw myself. It was as if I was now staring at a complete stranger, a body that I knew was my own form, but I did not feel that it was my own. I held up my hand and was quite surprised by the strange feeling that the hand just now looked like an object, it was familiar but there was no longer any sense of ownership.

I stared at the reflection of my form for some time and then began to notice that all of the mental noise that had until just moments before, plagued me, had now completely disappeared and that I found myself free from not only thoughts but suffering of any kind.

There was no judgement or attachment to anything, no resistance to life. Complete and thorough acceptance.

My mind was still capable of thinking but it was now as if the reins of the power of the mind were back in my control. Between my steady and *self-created* thoughts, just simple, profound and joyful stillness.

How had this been achieved I thought?

Surrender came the answer, but it was not answered as a thought, instead it was a deep 'knowing', complete and doubtless.

I had simply surrendered to the moment. I had given up wanting to fight it, fix it, change it or be anything other than just my self.

In a matter of moments, I had gone from being lost in depression, to seeing depression in myself but not being it, to being completely still, whilst the body recovered from its own sadness.

Now, as I stared at the relieved form reflecting back at me, I felt an incredible oneness with all of life. A feeling that I had encountered many times during peaceful Yogic meditation practices etc. but never on the receiving end of a massive suicidally-depressed and anxiety-ridden state.

Peace and joy filled my entire being. I felt that no longer was life *happening to me*. Life and I were one. I was the life of life itself.

The day continued in its beautiful form and although events occurred, I no longer saw them as favourable or undesirable, they just were. Judgements of the mind had ceased and instead a natural acceptance of life had replaced it. On some deeper level it was not even an acceptance. Life just was.

Even though there have been moments of emotions since in this body and times when mind has wandered off on its own. The feeling of being, not just that which is perceived, has never left. Conscious awareness once again found itself that morning and once this occurs, it can never go back. It is an irreversible awakening.

It was then, as I felt completely free from the suffering in which I had felt imprisoned in and by my own mind, that I realised that I had something to share with others who were also trapped in the confines of that which they thought they were.

Because it is only through that which 'we think we are' that our thoughts can appear to affect us or have any power over us. Once we get a glimpse of what we really are, this power diminishes and can never return to that level, even if the mind tries to make out that it can or it has.

Here lies your greatest strength. The knowledge that you too can access this. Surrender to the now and all that is, this is the key. Let yourself be free of time, be free of judgement of yourself or anything that you sense or perceive. Let it all just be. No judgement, no attachment and no resistance.

Once you have caught even the slightest glimpse of your true self, you will always know what it is to be free. You will always know the direction to follow, no matter how muddied or seemingly blocked the path.

This is both the beginning of the end and the end of the beginning. It is the start of your journey to freedom from all suffering. You will not just get your life back; you will realise you are life. Therefor one with all life and if you are one with all life, one with all that is, how can you not be free? How can you be anything other than at peace with what is? Because being against 'what is' is in essence what makes us suffer.

This is available to you. All it takes is an understanding, a desire and a willingness to maintain both of these. These aspects grow naturally as you begin to look within and recognise your own truth. This understanding also often requires following the pointings of someone who has already achieved this state of realisation.

*Were the jailers of my sanity (thoughts) really going to help me to get the keys? Or were they just playing a distraction game to keep me from seeing that the jail actually had no back wall.

Chapter One

IMPORTANCE OF GUIDANCE

THERE IS A WISE old saying which says "When the student is ready, the teacher will appear".

In life we often find that if we *go with the flow* of life it occurs from time to time that people or teachings will automatically enter our lives at a moment when we need them most.

This is especially true on the path to your true self.

In the early stages it may be a book, some videos on the internet or a meditation CD. As the journey progresses and as questions arise, it becomes very beneficial to have present someone who can guide you.

It is almost as if the teacher has returned back along the path, they once made through the thick jungle of unconsciousness and illusion to guide you down the same over-grown path, with their words of wisdom.

Following them in such a way, will not only help to remove the obstacles from your path, but it will assist you to overcome them when the time arrives.

Another yogic saying is that 'when the grass is tinder dry, only the smallest spark will ignite it'. When the teacher is present and the student is ready, it takes only the smallest application of energy to begin the burning which will transmute all that is unreal into the truth.

Having someone such as a yogi or spiritually awakened person present in your life, who knows the path, including all the pitfalls and joys to be found on that path, is an extremely valuable asset on the journey.

Quite often if you are able to have communication with them, they will be able to answer your questions and give direct guidance. However, they can also greatly assist you in finding that you have all of the answers in yourself.

Even the mere focus of our attention onto the one who has achieved awakening will help to 'still' the mind and bring focus and understanding of truth. In this way we can allow this focus to separate us from the distractions that may be disturbing our peace.

From the Hindu scripture the 'Bhagavad Gita' comes the saying 'Whosoever always and constantly thinks of Me, I am easily attainable'. Constant remembrance and attention towards the master and their teachings brings a never-ending peace.

This peace 'that passeth all understanding' is boundless, it knows no end.

When we hold a spiritually developed being, such as a yogi, in our attention we bring forth love, honour, faith, respect and surrender.

It is as though they, by your own focussed attention, have connected to your very heart centre and filled it with the pure divine love that they *know they are* and you will begin to experience as yourself also.

Whether the words and wisdom of our teachers reach us by being in direct contact with them, or without ever meeting the teacher through a CD recording, or through books; The guiding essence and grace that comes through these teachings is extremely valuable on the course towards recognition of our true self.

In this way we must not be disheartened, or feel like we cannot achieve freedom from suffering, if we do not have direct or personal access to our teachers. This can often be the way in which mind puts up a stumbling block to convince us that we are failing.

What we must instead recognise is that the power in the words of the teacher lie not in the words upon our senses but in the understanding in our heart. The greatest wisdom is felt as truth.

The application of such wisdom into our own existence is the fuel of awakening. Here we discover all the proof that is needed by applying that which a master has recognised to be *as it is.*

Often, we need not add anything into this *crucible of realisation* apart from our quiet attention, this is the catalyst for change, awareness and acceptance. The fire that heats the pot is the grace attached to the master's words. As their words are from pure consciousness, they are instantaneously endowed with the power of divine transformation.

I have been asked what it is like to have written a book, but the simple and truthful answer is that 'I' have not.

The words that have come through that which is being typed are very often unfamiliar later when proof read; as if reading the writing of another.

This is due to the words being gifted through this self, by that which exists in us both and all that is; Conscious awareness.

It is often said that it is ourselves that create our masters and teachings to awaken to that which we truly are.

All that is necessary for this to happen will 'step by step' make its way into your existence, as if you had carefully planned for it previously. This is why it is very important not to judge events, as often it will be the ones most challenging or confronting which have the biggest impact on our self-discovery.

Sometimes the words of a teacher will shine an intense 'spotlight' on the *falseness of that which you believe yourself to be*, that it will feel as though an accusation is almost made and you may want to run or hide from this intensity. This too is necessary. The words of the guru point so directly to truth that anything other than truth will feel rejected. This will often include the 'ego', which is that which your mind tells you that you are.

This is because one who has reached an awareness of a true self existing beyond minds interpretations, can often have a very direct way of communicating. They see themselves, their 'truth discovered', in you so strongly that they speak directly to that part of you. Which can offend the mind as it is very much accustomed to being spoken to as a person based on ego-mind.

In this way the teachings may seem harsh or unattainable. This can be because they are hard for the mind to understand. Here we need to allow the words just to be. Let the teachings simply be pointers to the truth. Let them wash over you or simply plant a seed of truth inside.

The more we can just be with the teachings of such a person, the more they will reveal of the being that they are and that which we are rediscovering.

They will often say or teach exactly what is necessary to alleviate and remove any illusion preventing the truth from being clearly seen, experienced or understood. This understanding is centred around becoming clear about what is our truth and what is not (illusionary). Beginning to understand how the mind creates these illusions, which in turn cause all of our suffering, is key here.

Chapter Two

STATES OF CONSCIOUSNESS

THE OM SYMBOL SYMBOLIZES four states of consciousness.

This includes the three normal states of everyday life that we all encounter; the most commonly experienced waking state, the dream state and the deep sleep state. We know that this last state happens, but are usually not aware of it so much due to lack of mental activity in this state.

What may a human expect to experience in each of these states?

In the deep sleep state, the mind is at rest completely. We are still conscious but, without the activity of the mind, deep sleep allows for a very peaceful state in which no projected thoughts of activity are present.

In the dream state the mind is active but the senses have been partially disabled by the body so that sleep and rest can still occur. The mind can now begin to act out thoughts and projections in a two-dimensional outlay in which the consciousness can be absorbed.

It is in this state that we begin to see just how incredible the mind is at creating. The dream creations of the mind, without sense, are so 'realistic' that perception becomes totally immersed in them. In this state we completely believe that the play of the mind, as the dream it has created, is our current reality. This is why nightmares are possible, it is our belief that they are real at that point in time, that we are actually suffering. It may also be a dream in which we are experiencing the opposite emotions and are immersed completely in the joy of the play of the mind.

Whatever the nature of the dream, the perception that we are the experiencer of the dream is something that is so overwhelmingly strong that it has our complete belief. That is until we awaken. Then it is merely seen as 'just a dream'. This may result in an instant feeling of relief, in the case of the nightmare, or of disappointment, in the case of the enjoyable dream experience. These sensations in the, newly attained, waking state are powerful indicators of our ability to be mislead by the minds 'stories'.

Once this realisation is seen, we very quickly lose the feelings and emotions that the dream had created. It loses a large portion of its reality. This is an important point to be remembered and noticed as often as possible because it in itself holds the key to unlock the secrets between other states. We will discuss this further.

It can happen that this actual realisation occurs during the dream itself whilst we remain in the sleep state, this is often called' lucid dreaming' and this gives the immediate ability for the awareness to become present in the dream and make the realisation that it is just that. This often finishes the dream and sometimes the sleep itself.

As we awaken and notice that all is back to normal, the dreams were just dreams, we (usually) are where we fell asleep, some time has passed but for us we had no awareness of what happen during that time whilst we were sleeping.

Our senses are what make us aware of all of this, we sense ourselves and our environment, our mind and senses work together at the speed of light building that which now seems so much more real than the dream. With all of the senses of touch, taste, smell, sight and sound active this which we now 'perceived' is even more believable than the two-dimensional play of the dream. We now have a three-dimensional masterpiece playing out and, due to its incredible realism and familiarity we instantly accept it as our reality.

With this added sense of realism we start to accept the fact that this is our life. It plays out in front of our senses and our mind makes countless interpretations through thoughts as to what it all means. We are now fully immersed in the daily projection and begin to have experiences which are usually based on events and our perceptions of such.

In this way we still experience both joy and suffering, but now, with the added enhancements of visual, audible and other sensory perception, at an even more believable level than that experienced during the dream state, in which we were completely deceived.

Is it possible there for that if we were so completely oblivious to the untrue nature of the dream, that in some way this waking state also is not exactly as it seems?

Could it be that we are also imbuing this state with an undeserved amount of belief?

In the dream state, was it not just a play in the mind? Yet how much do we believe it to be real? When we wake up, is it still real? It is easily seen to have been just a dream; a mind-made temporary belief which now no longer has any reality to it.

Is it possible that we may, as we did with the dream state, once again awaken into a different state in which we see that our mind has been merely telling us stories? As though we should wake up at least twice every day and also see that this is (the waking state), as seen from our belief as ourselves as a person, is also just another a play of the mind.

From a certain point of view, yes! It is possible!

If we are able to break free from the suffering feelings of a nightmare, by awakening (seeing it from a differing perception) then too it is completely possible for us to distance ourselves from the perception that these events in the waking state are actually 'happening to us'.

We can see this at the core of many of the teachings of the great spiritual teachers of the past and present. This 'awakening' is the essence of Buddha's enlightenment, of the Yogi's term Moksha and of the state of the 'kingdom of heaven' spoken about by Jesus.

So, if this 'fourth state' does exist, what is it? And how do we access it?

This state is called the 'Absolute'. It is pure awareness....

This absolute state or 'Turiya' is portrayed in the OM symbol as being above in the other states. In this state consciousness just is, regardless of mind or body activity.

In the OM symbol this final state is partitioned from the other normal states by a barrier which symbolises Maya, the mind made delusion that can keep us from experiencing that which we truly are.

This fourth state of consciousness pervades all of the other states, it lies in the background always. This is how we can 'know' that we had a good sleep, even if we did not dream.

It is our true self, known as 'Atman'. It is ever blissful, in harmony with all life, ever present, eternal. It is a place in which there is a conscious union between our self and all that is. From here all is witnessed in oneness and there for separation and suffering cannot occur.

So how do we access this state from the waking state? In the same way that we became aware that the dream we were believing in the dreaming state was not real; we have to realise that the projected play that we take as our experience in the waking state is also not quite as our mind would lead us to believe.

When we were lost in the dream state, we believed the dream to be entirely real. We can say that it was not real, that it was just a dream and that we became aware of this when we awoke to a new state. But what is also clear is that at the point of having the dream, it was the only reality that we had to believe in; or so our mind would lead us to believe.

But what was it that knew that we were dreaming? Was it not the same awareness that saw the mind think about it only being a dream when we had awakened?

Is it possible that underlying all of the three states there is a fourth state that never changes? One that witnesses all of these.

As we come to know that there is more to us than the mind would have us think, we start to find this fourth state. By shifting our attention into this state, we also begin to awaken from the belief that everything that mind tells us about this perceived reality is also not that much different from illusion of the dream.

In the dream state our mind creates and interprets events with incredible vivacity leaving us with little if any doubt that the events are actually occurring. Most of which the mind creates in the dream state is done in such a believable way that it is almost impossible to believe it not to be true. It may create conversations of friends or loved ones, even portraying their personality with seamless perfection. How does it do this?

If the mind is so capable of creating such believable imagery without senses, then what is it capable of creating with senses? Remembering that all of what we perceive in the waking state is only the minds interpretation of the messages sent to it from our senses.

If the mind was to misinterpret these messages it would make that which perceive as reality quite the opposite.

Our lives would there for then be perceived through a veil of mistruth. This is 'Maya' (or delusion) and it is the sole cause of all of the suffering in human life.

So how do we prevent this from continuing? As the dream state was brought to an end by the conscious arrival of the waking state, then so the potential disillusion of the minds interpretation of the waking state is brought to an end by the conscious awareness of the absolute. As we access this state by steadied awareness, we begin to see reality is not 'as we thought'.

Then, so as the emotions and feelings of the dream (or nightmare) quickly subdued as it was seen for what it was worth, so too does the harshness of the waking state (perceived reality) quickly diminish when it becomes apparent that most of it is purely the mind's interpretation.

By holding our beliefs firmly in the awareness of a state that exists beyond all of the other states, we remove all of our belief in any reality of these states. Without our belief they simply cease to exist, all that remains is the conscious awareness of the absolute itself (Turiya).

Hold firm your awareness of that which underlies all else.

It is your true nature.

This state of consciousness is free to be aware without any attachment. It merely witnesses all from a place of peaceful, blissful conscious awareness. One with existence.

Chapter Three

WITNESS CONSCIOUSNESS

WITHOUT YOUR CONSCIOUSNESS WHERE would the existence of 'all this in the phenomenal world' be? Is it not your consciousness that allows all this to be? If it was not for your perception, it would just be countless atoms and space.

When we are in the sleep state, we still remain conscious, if a loud noise was to occur or someone was to shake us our consciousness would shift from the dream, we may have been having to the room we are sleeping. We would be aware that just moments ago we were still here but yet sleeping soundly or watching a dream. This background consciousness is a wonderful clue to that which enables existence not just of the dream state but also of the waking state. Similarly, in the deep sleep state we may have no mind activity but there is a part of us that still remains, it is this that we speak of as 'having had a good sleep'.

This conscious awareness remains at all times. It is why we have (and more accurately) *are* life!

Most of our life is spent in the waking state and as such it is key here to begin to see that this consciousness, which exists and enables dream states and all they contain, is also present as that in which the waking state unfolds. It simply is.

You are the witness consciousness, not indifferent from universal consciousness itself, witnessing the dream or play of forms that consciousness itself projects. Know this to be yourself.

In this way, all that we are conscious of, is reflected back unto consciousness itself as would a city reflected in a mirror. A city never acts, does or even believes itself to be a city, it simply is. If it were to see itself in a mirror it may be aware of activity, but all that happens is just part of what makes it a city. Similarly, that part of you which can reflect upon itself in your truest form *just is*, even though it may appear as magnificent and active, beyond this, it simply just is. With this knowing we no longer wrongly perceive ourselves to be that which plays out the play, but the audience at one with the theatre in which the play occurs.

As a witness of consciousness, you are formless, endless, nameless, timeless.

Here there is no attachment to forms, no attachment to time, no beginning/no end, it was not born and cannot die!

Blissful joy arises from the knowledge of yourself as the existence only of consciousness.

You free yourself from any desires or aversions to events, outcomes or objects. You now flow free like a previously drowning man who surrenders to the awesome power of the "riptide". Instead of trying to swim with all his might against its unfathomable power, he just relaxes and allows the flow to lead him back to calmer waters.

If you focus your energy on the belief that you are a person you will strengthen the belief and the personhood. If you place your attention on the perceiver or the witness of the person you will strengthen that and the personhood will disappear or merge.

If you wait for the person to disappear you are once again placing attention and strength into it. Instead, just know the person to be *just a belief* (the thoughts of who you are) by instead being the perceiver of the person.

Begin to notice that this sense of self is temporarily empowered or given existence by creating thoughts of who it is. It may say "oh you failed the driving test again" that makes 'me' a bad driver! It now has more of a sense of self.

It will even try to add to that by continuing the thoughts down the track, "Why should I book another driving test I am never going to pass it! Because I am a bad driver."

The thought of never going to pass it is added to the concept of bad driver. As will be any mistakes made, even if you pass.

What has to be noticed here is that the thought 'I am a bad driver' is just that, a thought. But when you think about it and give it chance to exist it becomes that which you think you are: Me, myself and I.

Any thoughts that attach to it are again just thoughts. They have no substance apart from your belief in them.

If you place your belief in the fact that you are the attention witnessing 'just' thoughts! Then they will immediately lose power, as will your sense of self.

Self-confidence is a good thing to have to an extent, but once again if you believe yourself to be a good driver (which is better than believing yourself to be a bad driver) you have still created a sense of self which is based purely on a thought.

In this case you may derive some pleasure, attachment and further sense of self from this thought. So, caution here is needed. Thinking yourself to be a great driver, what would then happen if you accidentally lost control and drove into a street pole? Are you now a bad driver? Will your mind try and tell you so? Yes. Because your investment in being a driver, good or bad, is heavily based on previous thoughts.

What do you do then?

You stay as the true self. The now, the isness. You do not label yourself as any type of driver. You just drive. Surrendering the action of driving to life by remaining within your 'witnessing self'.

Awakening is the recognition, remembrance and rediscovering of your self in its purest form.

Enlightenment is staying in this purest form.

As you stay in this, so your believed self begins to disappear. A love for this is-ness begins to grow as it alone consists of purest freedom from suffering. This love blends in with the love that it is and the love of all that is.

Soon life loses all of its harshness. All of its ups and downs. Peace pervades. Bliss becomes the natural outcome of all that is.

Once again though be aware that even *all of this* is just witnessed. From this witness point oneness with creation is discovered.

How do we then stop mind from returning and taking control of our life with various thoughts? We remain vigilant, being aware of our thoughts; but most importantly we continue to resist the desire to believe the minds continuous interpretations. Seeing them also as just passing thoughts.

As we will see, this is of paramount importance.

Chapter Four

PLACING ZERO VALUE IN THOUGHTS - THE GOLDEN KEY

IF WE MOMENTARILY CONSIDER the story of the fictional character Tony Stark who goes on to become 'Iron Man'. He is portrayed as a character who personally witnesses the atrocities being caused by the weapons his own company supplies. They are being used to destroy the innocent and cause terror.

If we look at this from another perspective, we can begin to see a similarity between this and the potential destruction that can be created by the mind, which is using the beliefs and judgements that we supply it.

As Tony Stark decides that no longer will Stark Industries create weapons for supply, therefore removing the capabilities of the terror causing organisations. We too can remove the minds ability to cause fear, destructive thoughts and patterning by removing our value of it.

It needs this belief to cause pain, without it, it is like a fangless snake.

Do not give the thoughts of the mind any value. Do not judge them. Do not get involved with them. Feed it nothing and witness its damaging powers completely disappear. Only through the power we invest in it can mind have any power of itself. It has no power of its own.

Ok, so if this is the answer itself to the freedom from all of our suffering…. how do we do this?

As we would a bully in a school yard. By beginning to ignore its antics, see it for what it is and not be afraid of it.

We have likely all encountered a bully at school or elsewhere. A bully is often a character who loves to be noticed and make themselves seem greater by making others suffer and feel less. A bully will spend much of their time belittling and threatening, even physically fighting to prove their strength. A strength they usually actually lack and are desperate to portray as being present. They usually have a lot of fears within themselves about not being good enough with very low actual self-belief and so they go around making others feel 'less' to make themselves feel 'more'.

So how does this concept of a bully help with freedom from suffering?

If we look at what it is that gives the bully his/her power and believed strength, it becomes apparent that without the ability to be-little others and gain power from it, from causing others to be fearful or feel less, they lose the ability to gain power. Their imagined power begins to disappear.

If a bully in a school yard 'picks' on a particular child one day who is equally strong or stronger and fails to cause fear, then their ability to be a 'bully' begins to rapidly disappear. At this point most of the kids who were previously getting bullied begin to realise that the bully is not as strong as they had thought. Now if the bully tries to continue their fear creating antics, the others start to ignore the bully, they place less interest in his/her actions and immediately the bully's source of power (that in which they're feared) is quickly removed.

So too with the ego-mind. As we see in the example of the 'schoolyard' with the bigger kid, we may witness something stronger (more powerful) that exists, alleviating us of our fears. In this case, something more than the troublesome mind; which is our true self. In witnessing this, we start to remove the power that the mind has to cause destructive (negative) thoughts and fear by removing our value in its thoughts; by starting to see it for what it is and ignoring it.

Our suffering, our mental crises, that which we perceive as wrong or unfavourable, which is 'happening' to us; all of this comes from our identity with and our belief in our thoughts.

None of this is possible unless we identify with our thoughts in such a way that we believe we are the thoughts themselves or a 'persona' which believes that these thoughts are what makes us 'who we are'.

They are given unnecessary value and subsequent power that they do not deserve.

In return they bolster a sense of self. That who we 'think' we are.

Are they not just thoughts?

If you think something bad about yourself, life (past/future) or your current situation, is it not a simple telling of the mind, no different to that which perceives a kitten to be cute or a wind to be cold. They are all just mental perceptions.

Yet once we over-emphasise their importance, the power they have becomes personal and it is this alone which creates all of the suffering in the world today. I do not say this lightly.

The mind of man has the innate ability to individualise itself completely. This creates a sense of separation and a feeling of 'I am all on my own' even when it is clear the person is not. All number of sufferings stem from this belief that we are separate from all else that is.

How do we step away from this and give it the space and distance required for us to see this?

What is needed is the realisation that we are not what we think of. Thoughts are just that, mental imageries. They exist inside of us, but can only exist because of what we truly are, silent awareness. Alternatively, the awareness can exist without the thoughts, as is clearly evident in the state of deep sleep, when we are still here but mind itself is completely inactive.

Let the thoughts be. Do not give them any value. Let them float across the mind like a cloud crosses the sky. Set yourself free from the belief that thoughts make you what you are. Know yourself to be that which exists in the moments before and after each thought. It cannot be otherwise.

Here you will find peace. Stillness. Clarity. Truth. Wisdom. Love.

But most importantly you will cease to believe that you are separate and alone.

You will begin to see that you are no different to life itself. That which exists in everything, including all events and all others.

As you begin to find the peace and essence of your own being, so to will you begin to see that peace and beingness in all others. This creates oneness with life itself and all within it. What greater goal for a human life?

The manifestation of thoughts to events also can occur through belief and value of thoughts.

The formless becomes form due to a focussing of perception, a 'concentration of belief'. Just as the power of the sun's rays can be intensified by the use of a magnifying glass, the mind's thoughts can be magnified into events by the action of value and belief in them. Removing the belief is like removing the magnifying glass, it prevents the thoughts from becoming more than they are.

To enable us to maintain a clear distance from our thoughts and prevent unnecessary belief in them. We need to develop a stillness of the mind. We need to be able to 'find the gaps' that exist between thoughts and let this be our normal resting place. From here we will clearly develop the ability to notice the activity of the mind, but remain a witness to its activity.

There are many ways to reach this state. Meditation can be of the greatest assistance. Meditation is achievable by all. It is simply any number of ways to achieve a recognition of minds activities and that which also continues to exist whilst mind is not active.

This is how meditation allows us to bot recognise what we are not and rediscover what we truly are.

Chapter Five

MEDITATION AND STILLNESS

WHEN STARTING ON THE road to bliss of peaceful meditation, it is often the case that silence enables us to have the peace of mind conducive to this discovery.

Often the meditation that occurs in silence is the one that enables us to achieve greatest recognition of the emptiness of thought in which our true self resides.

As time and our spiritual growth progresses, we begin to find that we no longer need this silence to achieve peace. Meditation can occur at any time during the day, despite the background noise or activity.

In fact, something even more astounding starts to occur; we now find that the bliss of being, instead of occurring easier due to silence, is actually creating silence. Sometimes this can occur as a diminishing of sounds and activity but mostly it occurs as a peacefulness which covers all around you, almost like a blanket of snow brings pure white to all it gently falls upon.

These stories from my own personal experience may help to give you some idea of how this may occur.

Many years ago, I had the opportunity to attend a one-on-one meditation session with a Yogi affectionately named 'Swamiji' who was over in Australia staying with his family.

I was honoured and a little nervous as having never done anything like this. When I arrived at the house, I was invited in and told it would not be long before Swamiji would see me.

He entered the room soon after and greeted me and took a seat on a cushion in front of me. I sat down on the floor in similar position and he began to talk a little about his teachings and the meditation we would conduct.

It was a very hot day and one the family members came in to the room and asked if we wanted a fan on. A large fan was brought in and turned up high, whirring audibly. It was very strong and it made the window blinds on the other side of the room clatter loudly also.

I sat in a cross-legged position to mirror the master in front of me and listened intently to the master.

After some time, we began the meditation and I closed my eyes, it was a non-verbal meditation, so after a small prayer of intent no other speaking occurred.

As I sat, I began to notice that throughout the rest of the house lots of other noises were occurring. They had been there before but now I noticed them clearly as we had stopped speaking.

General sounds of a family household were evident like kitchen noises, pots and pans being moved, drawers and cupboards closing. A T.V. could be heard and some music maybe from a radio. People talking and small children excitedly calling out and moving around.

Adding to this was the noise of the fan and blinds. It was very unlike the normal quiet settings that I had usually meditated in up to this point.

My mind was wandering, distracted by all of the activity.

I also began to notice that due to having sat so long cross legged up to this point I now found that my legs were getting a lot of pins and needles and starting to get sore.

The further time went on the worse things got, the heat of the room meant sweat was pouring down my face. Small children would ride into the room and come up close to me all whilst lots of noises continued to get louder and my legs ached more and more.

I was not sure how long it had been or how much further we had to go but all I could do in respect for this great master was just sit and suffer in silence.

I wondered how we was able to find peace in amongst all the noise.

More and more time went by and I thought it could not end fast enough. Then, just as I felt as though I would pass out from pain in my legs, I had the thought that I cannot change what is, I have no control over what is happening and was not going to move my legs even if I could, so I just surrendered to the situation.

I gave up wishing for it to be different. I accepted it as it was, the pain, the heat, the noise, the apparent distractions.

Then something very strange happened. My mind suddenly slowed to a stop. It stopped judging the situation and events. It became still and my focus of attention went from outside and all the sensory perceptions to inside and the stillness that existed here.

The meditation continued for quite some time longer and then at the end the master uttered the sacred word "Aum" to signify the end of the meditation.

It was at this point that my mind returned and was instantly aware that the house had fallen into a noticeable stillness, the fan was still blowing at the same speed but it no longer seemed harsh, the blinds chattered but gently. All of the voices and noises of the house had disappeared and it remained as if now empty. My legs no longer hurt and the room felt significantly cooler.

It occurred to me at this point that it was almost as though our meditation had created the stillness in which we sat and yet I had always been so used to it being the other way around.

Another similar experience of acceptance and the emergence of silence from within, despite the noise outside, occurred some years after.

One morning I was holidaying with my family in the beautiful port town of Fremantle in Western Australia. I woke early and went for a walk up a mounded hill on top of which is an old convict building called 'The Roundhouse'. There was a small park bench atop the hill and I sat to rest and closed my eyes. From the nearby ocean I could hear the sounds of peaceful waves crashing and Seagulls calling. The wind was gently blowing a cool breeze and I soon entered a very beautiful meditative state.

After some time, I heard the voices of some people approaching, my senses were aware of them, as I was aware of the other sounds, but my attention remained fixed in the stillness of the moment.

I was a 'witness only' to both my thoughts and any processing of external sensory perceptions.

As the pedestrians approached, I became aware that there were two voices, both male and they were in a very aggravated conversation about driving in morning traffic. The words were harsh and loud. Yet I remained still, accepting and witnessing all without judgement.

The path which they were walking was the one I had followed and it led right in front of where I was sitting. I cannot remember the exact words but the dialogue of the conversation as they passed me was similar to this, "I went down 'so and so' street and got stuck behind every f-ing slow person!", followed by "Yeah, I copped every single f-ing traffic light!".

I remained eyes closed in a deep meditative state with attention fully focussed on being and witnessing only. My mind was processing and detecting but it and its thoughts, were watched peacefully from a non-attached point of view.

After the passers-by had continued to walk away down the path back down the hill, I opened my eyes slowly and looked around at the beautiful scenery which lay in front of me looking out across the ocean, my gaze went towards the two men who were nearly out of sight. It was at this moment that one of the men turned back and looked straight at me for a couple of seconds silently before turning back the way he was walking.

I felt deep inside that a part of this man had noticed my stillness and through all of his own mental noise, some quiet part of himself had recognised itself and wanted to glance back, to acknowledge this recognition.

Even though, when the two people had walked past me, we had been in quite opposite states of mind, a frequency of silent stillness had become aware of itself throughout all of the noise.

Frequent meditation will help you to access this state more and more easily in all situations, after achieving awareness of the silent stillness of the witness consciousness you are – that which is called 'Atman'. Stay with this and not only be with it, but be it.

Become aware of what it is like to be fully present and yet not be overwhelmed by unwanted thoughts. Envelope yourself in the peace. This true peace cannot be disturbed.

After meditation, thoughts may try to come when you open your eyes etc. but the peace remains within. Practice this on a daily basis if possible. You will notice that the thoughts that try to distract you are about the false self, or about things that have happened in the past or may happen in the future. These may be self-judgements, regrets or fears. The ego mind utilises them as a powerful crowbar to lever you from your peace.

But as you remain firmly established in the awareness that 'you are the peace' and that there is only now, thoughts such as these have no power, they are recognized to be completely illusory.

Resting in your beingness prevents you from being affected by the mind made suffering. The more time you spend in it the more of an immunity it builds. The beingness coats you as does the oil on a water bird so that no matter how far you plunge into the depths of life, when you surface the water just runs off. You stay dry, unaffected.

In this 'peace of mind' you will find that more and more you begin to recognise the permanent nature of your stillness and the contrasting impermanence of thoughts, emotions and in fact everything other than your stillness. All things come and go except your true self, but this is hardly surprising as your true self is not a 'thing' at all. It is that in which all things occur and exist. It alone is that which remains always.

Chapter Six

IMPERMANENCE

AWARENESS OF IMPERMANENCE IS a very useful tool along the journey. When we start to accept that all things are impermanent it not only helps with a reduction in attachment, but it also helps us to realise that there is something that witnesses all this impermanency; something permanent. Something eternal.

Only that which is permanent can witness impermanency. Only that which exists always can have awareness of that which does not.

The attachment to things, which includes everything we can witness, often revolves around the need for 'this thing' to last forever. This comes from an early age as we feel the apparent pain of loss when something we invest part of ourselves into is removed from our lives.

We have relationships with things, which also includes other people and animals etc. We also have a relationship with that which we take ourselves to be; Our body-mind intellect. When threatened with the loss of any of these we encounter fear and subsequent suffering. However, we find it very hard to not keep re-attaching ourselves to new things.

If we begin to become aware of the impermanence of all things, including relationships and the birth to death governed lives of our self and others, then we start to relinquish these fears and release the potential suffering.

Of course, we do not have to visit a cemetery to do this, although that may be of benefit at some stage to help see the fleetingness of that which call life, but we can start with noticing simple things.

We sleep, but not forever, we wake and sleep is done. Impermanent.

We sit in a traffic jam, but not forever, we get where we are going and the traffic is a memory. Impermanence.

We think a bad thought, feel a bad emotion, or suffer a panic attack. They pass and go. They do not last forever.

From noticing these small day-to-day changes, we start to become aware of that that which changes and that which is changeless, this is a very good way of beginning to see the truth of which you are.

As time goes on you can apply this practice to greater things that may have caused you some resistance in the past or cause great suffering.

Life will no longer appear as though it is being overly troublesome, problematic or even vengeful. Events will come and go. More and more you will be in a place of silent eternal witnessing. Dramas will not fill you with dread. 'This too will pass' will become your wise motto.

All things are impermanent. Except that which is no thing; nothingness. From this place all can be perceived as coming and going. Like clouds in the sky. You are the sky.

Let all things come and go. Do not try to change this. This is how acceptance, non-resistance and non-judgement can be very powerful tools which you can acquire, practice and eventually become very skilful at using.

They enable you keep a distance from thoughts and occurrences, without a sense of personal involvement. This then allows you to move amongst life without it sticking to you. Things just come and go. You do not derive a sense of self from them or look to them for confirmation of who you are.

You remain a silent witness. This place of unaffected witnessing is always here. It cannot leave you or be apart from you.

Allowing your attention to rest peacefully in this 'ever-present' state of just being, you will begin to not only recall and rediscover what it was like to just 'be', but because of the unending joy, peace and love that naturally emanates from this state, you will also recognise it more and more as the only way of life.

It simply is.

Effortless.

Chapter Seven

BALANCE

THE 'MIDDLE PATH' IS a term that was used by Buddha.

It means taking a path that is neither extremely adverse or one that is overly nonchalant, neither too strict or too unruly.

Buddha proposed this way of living after trying many different forms of techniques and practices in his search for inner peace and an understanding to life and freedom from its sufferings.

The knowledge that he gained through experience of these practices lead him to the realisation that a middle way should be sought in living a life where peacefulness and freedom of suffering is the desired destination. He believed that one should not attempt to undertake any extreme practices to advance your spiritual progression. Instead you should maintain a natural path of mediocrity, in this way we begin to find ourselves able to relax more and 'enjoy the ride'.

Putting high demands upon yourself as a 'spiritual seeker' who needs to perform rigorous spiritual practice all day, every day for years can actually restrict progress. It can empower the ego by harbouring thoughts of needing more, of not being enough.

Regular practices such as meditation etc. can of course be very beneficial on the path to awakening, but again moderation is the key. With such moderation in our meditation practice, it enables us to assimilate the meditative learnings.

In fact, moderation and balance are the essence of the teaching of the middle path. Having a healthy balance of practice and non-practice is an example of what Buddha meant when he speaks of this middle path or middle way. If you were to continuously meditate, then how could the wisdom of this meditation be of any benefit to yourself or others in your daily existence. It may remove the suffering from yourself for that time you meditate but no person is capable of meditating forever, we need to sleep, drink, eat etc.

Adversely, not performing any practice would be similar to an athlete turning up to a competitive event without conducting any prior training and still expecting the event to be an easy win.

Applying moderation to other areas of your day-to-day life can also assist in finding a smooth path.

The Sanskrit word Sattva is one of the three guṇas or qualities. It is defined by peace and harmony but also by balance. A Sattvic lifestyle is one in which balance is brought in to all areas of living. Sleeping, eating, activities etc.

One should look to get enough sleep; this is naturally hard to formally address as it can change due to a number of factors such as age etc. But what is necessary is to make sure that you give your body chance to sleep long enough and not force your body to keep sleeping if it wakes after suitable sleep.

Eating is another very important area of our lives which can often play a large part in finding inner harmony. If we eat too little our bodies will not have the energy to perform other actions which may assist in keeping moderation such as exercise etc. However, if we eat too much our bodies may become lethargic or unhealthy also making these activities again difficult to accomplish. A lack of moderation in eating, especially certain food, can also lead to over-activity in the mind.

Sattvic diets can also assist here, but again there must be a balance in eating satisfactorily.

It can be the case that certain foods affect certain people in such a way that they have a very negative effect on maintaining a clear mind, free from over-activity of thoughts. Such foods can include Garlic and Onion. Dietary advice can be sought, however it can also be possible to abstain from certain foods for a while and see what benefit or affect this has.

Activity is not only healthy for the body but also for the mind. It can bring about stillness within the body if conducted from a place of witnessing. This does not have to be intense bodily workouts but can be as simple as going for a nice early morning walk.

Bringing this Sattvic balance into one's life will not only bring about harmony in ones own physical and mental states but it will also start to ease the need for extremes of events and actions to be satisfying.

In this way you will begin to see that it is the simple things in life which hold the greatest reward.

What you are in essence doing is using your will power over and over again, to make your day the way you wish for it to be, to be most beneficial for your own growth. In this way you strengthen your own spiritual fortitude. Which in turn will enable you to glide through life's challenging times with an ever-increasing grace.

Your mind will lose its ability to continually grab your attention and you will find more and more peace and harmony within yourself as your self.

As the noisiness of the mind quietens, you will become aware of another source of information. But where the mind was based on acquired knowledge; this other source appears to have no knowledge base.

More and more will you begin to do that which is necessary to align yourself with life, as a seeming voice of grace and wisdom becomes that which you listen to more than the noisy and needy constant chatter of the mind.

You will find that 'right action' occurs with greater frequency in your life and emanates out affecting the lives of many others in a truly magnificent way, as you begin to listen to this inner voice of wisdom.

As you progress on towards the rediscovery of your truth, on the subtlest level you will become aware that you are no different to 'life itself'. With this realisation will also come the understanding that if you are *one with life* then it is only natural that you have all of the wisdom within you already to enable choices and decisions which perpetually correlate and align with life.

In this way you begin to trust your own innate ability to understand what is required to maintain this balance and 'middle path'. This is intuition and it is your greatest asset. Once you understand how it works, trust it and let it guide your decisions, it will never fail you.

Chapter Eight

INTUITIVE KNOWING

THERE IS A PART of you that knows exactly what you will need for the future. If you pick up four loaves of bread at the supermarket and a little voice appears out of nowhere and says take five, then take five. When a whole bunch of friends unexpectedly arrive for a lunch soon thereafter then you will find that extra loaf and all will be as it should be.

The more that you begin to 'trust' this intuitive knowing, the clearer it will be to 'hear' this little voice and the more often it will appear to *assist*. It is the same 'gut feeling' that tells you to slow down in your car in a way that assists you to avoid an accident, which would have occurred at your previous speed.

This part of you is completely at 'one with all that is', it there for has unlimited access to life before it even manifests into existence.

How do you know that it is your intuition, rather than mental thoughts? Both exist as consciousness. But as the mind-based thoughts are like waves on the surface of the ocean, your true guidance comes from the deep, ever-stillness of the ocean itself. Mind-based thoughts will often be associated with emotions, such as fear or neediness whereas intuitiveness comes almost as a feeling itself, it just is. There is a momentum behind it.

Along the course of the journey this intuition can play many parts. All of which reinforce your understanding of your true self by giving you glimpses of a force inside of you which has an undeniable and also unthinkable access to knowledge and wisdom of which you never 'knew' existed.

At the beginning the simple recognition of a part of you that may know or have known better in any particular situation will begin to unlock the power of this guidance. It may be that at first you often say "I just knew that was going to happen" or "I knew I should not have done that", referring to a particular feeling that you may have had before an event and did or did not act upon. It matters not that you did not pay attention to the feeling at first, only that you were aware of it.

As time goes on, more and more will the feeling and 'knowing' re-occur once it has found a part of your attention and as your mind becomes less noisy; which allows the subtle intuitive voice to be more clearly heard.

Eventually you will learn to listen more to this intuition and as a reward for this you will see and feel that you begin to take a less painful pathway. Life seems to be come very favourable.

This will continue and as you evolve a time will come when it will simply become 'second nature'.

At this part of the journey this is very important to help with seeing that within you is a wisdom and understanding which can assist in enabling a life free from suffering.

One thing to be careful of here is the pitfall of becoming arrogant and building up your ego with thoughts such as I always make the best decisions; simply just let them play out and be grateful. It is at this point that we need to begin to 'action for the sake of actioning', righteously, allowing outcomes to *just be* with no personal attachment to them. These actions can be now safely done in the knowledge that right action is taking place due to *trust* in intuition.

Continuing on from here you will come to a point when it is no longer necessary to action this or that. This is very advanced in the journey and occurs at a time when no longer is there a need for outcomes to 'play out' in any particular way.

No longer will intuition feel like something separate or different; it will be the grace that flows through you into everything that occurs.

This awareness of the ability of grace, life force or whatever you want to call it, to flow into existence can also be 'bottled and gifted' if required.

Although much of the goodness that comes from utilisation of intuitive action flows directly to our self or others without request or direction, it is possible and very beneficial to direct the potential benefits of this good intent.

Chapter Nine

SELFLESS INTENT

PRAYER HAS A BIT of a stigma that it is something that can only be done by someone of a religious or very spiritual background. This is not the case. Prayer or as I prefer to call it 'Selfless intent' does not even need to be religious at all and many non-god believing people successfully make a wishful heartfelt request come true each and every day.

This selfless intent does not mean that one has to find a quiet place, kneel, placing hands together in a certain way or direction or any of that (but if that is how you pray then that is fine also).

It is simply giving a silent, written or spoken intent of that which is something you believe would be beneficial if it were to manifest in this life. It can be for yourself, for others, for the planet or anything. This positive power of intent, lets life know that which you truly wish to attract into existence.

Offering this pure intent for yourself or others can be extremely beneficial because it helps to create a flow of positive karma just by the intent itself. This will not only flow out to the recipient in the form of best wishes but in some way will also return to yourself. Keeping in mind that a prayer made just to receive self-benefits will not be rewarded in kind. Here 'selflessness intent' is paramount.

When we sit silently and allow our heart to speak with life through prayer, we allow ourselves to be truly connected. It allows us to re-unite with divine presence and creation. The word 'Yoga' has the meaning 'reunion with the divine'. So, the divinity in ourselves and that of creation itself become one, as does the water in a river flowing back into the sea from where it once came.

This connective occurrence within prayer is greatly beneficial as it enables our self to once again witness itself reflected as all that is; all the while learning of its inherent creationary abilities.

In our spiritual practice, 'selfless intent' can be of great benefit. When we find ourselves in a state of heightened awareness, consciousness, peace and serenity it is often extremely beneficial to confirm this joy by giving thanks by prayer and intent for this particular experience to continue, grow and flourish. Meditation is often followed by this respectful prayer to the grace which flows as you in that state. Gratefully and open for further continuance.

Give intent that this awareness and your establishment within it continues.

Loving intent given for others who are in need of freedom from mental, emotional or physical suffering is of the highest degree. It is a beautiful way of sending grace and assistance to those who need it most, even those that we cannot physically attend.

Intent for specific favourable outcomes can of course be conducted, but it would be wise to abstain from needfully requiring particular events to occur. This can lead to attachment and suffering. Instead, it would be more beneficial to just hold in one's thoughts the knowing that whatever occurs regarding this event all will be as it should; perfectly. Here lies great power, allowing life and the grace that flows into existence to act in accordance with pure creation.

It is of far greater importance to 'wish well' in a prayer than to request particular outcomes. As these outcomes may not be in accordance with divine will and this will mean that you are not aligning yourself with life. This does not mean that your positive thoughts will have any affect, they too are part of the influence of direction, but an agenda for all existence is also occurring.

To wish a person or situation well works divinely because it projects from your heart and is also reflected back to your heart. This is why it feels so good to let someone know that you are thinking of them in a challenging time.

Prayers are simply that, positive thoughts of well-being.

They are both symbols and gifts of loving kindness. They never miss their mark. They are also always reciprocated in some way or another, even if unknowingly returned through karmic events.

It is important to note here again that the utilisation of intent should always be selfless, so as to not have any 'personal' gain as this would not only be directed from the ego, but be utilised by the same for some kind of self-inflation.

It is also important to not rely on particular outcomes from intent as these come again with a personal desire; which can again lead to suffering in the form of disappointment etc. if the desired outcome does not eventuate. Selfless intent or prayers are not wishful thinking they are gifts of love, kindness and compassion. They work because they are free from attachment or judgement of potential 'right or wrong'.

Chapter Ten

NON-LABELLING/
NO JUDGEMENT
REVISITING JAR

IF WE JUDGE AN object as bad because of our interpretation of it then we sometimes overlook the actual
potential beauty of that which we perceive. For example,
the fruit 'Durian' is infamous for being a very smelly
fruit. It is even banned from being carried on part of the
Singapore public transport system because of this reason.
However, it is believed by many to be one of the tastiest
fruits, with a sweet palatable taste.

It could be the case that many people have never tasted
this fruit purely because it smells 'bad' or that they are
told it does. Our judgements of what is bad and good
are sometimes based on what we experience, but are also
often reliant on the judgements of others. We therefor

spend a lot of our time judging and labelling based on what others believe.

Is it possible that there is actually no good or bad?

That everything is just exactly as it is supposed to be?

It has been said by the yogis that all things even those we label as very unpleasant, such the odour of faeces, are actually not bad and that its smell is actually as it should be. This also applies to the non-labelling of events as bad, such as a terrible crime. The being that sees truth in all things from the inner rediscovered truth of themselves, has overcome the need to judge anything as unfavourable, everything is at it should be. This is complete freedom from judgement.

So, what is the importance of freedom from judgement? Simply, without judgement there can be no suffering. Suffering occurs because we value the minds interpretation of an event as undesirable. If we see everything as 'being as it should be', not good or bad, no judgement, then suffering will not occur.

This can be challenging at the start of the journey as it has been a very important part of our 'growing up' to assess things as good or bad and to use this to create a list of *right* and *wrong*. We have become, not only very used to, but also very reliant on this judgement to coordinate what is favourable.

Walking barefooted across a particular patch of grass known for its prickles will often produce the same outcome. In this case we have assessed the outcomes and added the potential event into the unfavourable list.

However, a time may come when, after being very engrossed in a conversation whilst walking barefooted across the same patch of grass, you forget and again get a bad prickle in your feet. The person who you were talking to just happens to have strong feelings for you in a romantic way of which you were unaware (but felt reciprocally) and this opportunity enables them to show how much they care for you and enables a potentially life-changing relationship to grow from this (literal) point onwards.

This is a sign of how things that occur should not be labelled as definitively good or bad. In this case you may say I am so glad I stepped on that prickle and it could make the whole *prickle thing* and the list of right or wrong seem very cloudy indeed.

When we start to look at life like this we can, not only see it occur more and more in our daily lives but also; see it having occurred many times in our past, which possibly lead to favourable outcomes even though at the time the event was considered 'bad'.

Again, more and more, as we notice this occurrence and discover within ourselves a greater *acceptance of life*; we begin to see that judgement of life is no longer necessary. It all just is; as it should be, always.

With this awareness now becoming firmly set in our hearts we drop the need for events to occur in particular ways. When events do occur, they begin to lose the offending harshness and power that they can have over us.

Sometimes the news can be very emotionally draining, often due to the alluring and attention-grabbing nature of 'bad news'. Much of the news which is published or presented is of this type.

However bad news for some can be good news for others, constant rain over a long weekend can drown out plans for particular festivities but cause elation for drought-stricken farmers.

Pandemic outbreaks of viruses can cause much angst, fear and anger etc. But they can also bring people closer together, reduce pollution and harmonise the world with compassion towards each other.

The reduction of judgement, as well as non-resistance of life and reduction of attachments, which are all interlinked, is not only something that you can work on throughout the journey but also a beautiful gift returned to you as the journey continues.

You will find that not only are you impacted less by occurrences for which you now no longer judge, but you will also judge your self less. Placing less judgement on your own actions can help to alleviate many of the causes of personal suffering.

It also helps you to begin to distance yourself, from any personal attachment, to the outcome of your actions. This does not mean you can go around doing what is humanely regarded as unacceptable. It means that the responsibility for personally 'doing' lessens, as the witnessing presence of 'being' increases as life unfolds.

When this occurs and you become aware of it, it will reinforce your understanding of that which you are, life itself.

Chapter Eleven

EQUANIMITY

FINDING PEACE IN ALL moments depends on our ability to 'just be'. Letting it (life) be, free from personal interpretations, allows us to just be also. When we are just being, there is nothing that can affect us in any way. Our beingness exists in a realm or dimension in which there are 'no things'; all are just perceptions in the dream and waking states. In deep sleep, mind is inactive so no perceptions exist, it should be noted that *here* we are in a natural state of beingness also.

One of the ways to achieve this 'being in your beingness' in the dream and waking states, especially during times when it feels like the waves of the mind are crashing down in a seemingly rough sea of consciousness, is to keep coming back to neutrality or evenness in the mind.

Maintaining equanimity is a key to opening the doors to freedom from suffering. The correct word for this in Buddhist teaching is Upekkhā. It basically means letting go or to 'over look'. This in itself sounds like you must then have a 'don't care' attitude but this could not be further from the truth.

When we begin to nurture a mind that is neutral, through the practice of meditation, we begin to see all that is, is as it should be. We hold no judgements. We simply let it be. In allowing this to happen our mental state rises above that in which thoughts have the ability to taint our existence. A neutral mind does not get involved in the battles and wars that surround it. It remains in the peace that it has chosen.

Equanimity is a word that is derived from the Latin words for 'even' and 'mind'. Even-mindedness is a by-product of consistent meditation. Through the flowering of stillness of mind during meditation the fruits begin to bear during existence *outside of the meditation practice*. This neutrality is one of them, it is essential for letting go, letting life be and has a key part to play in being free to be you.

One who has equanimity is suddenly freed from the attacking interpretations of the noisy mind. This is because equanimity occurs at a place where there are no points of 'self-reference'. Then events cannot be taken personally as they have no direction or subsequent anchor points to self. They simply cannot attach to that which you imagine is what makes up 'your life', that which makes up how, who, why, when and what you are.

What is important to remember here is that mind is just consciousness. During meditation we allow the mind to still itself. It can be imagined that if the mind is the wild surface waters of a tumultuous sea, stillness of pure consciousness is the motionless waters below unaffected by wind and weather above.

What happens during equanimity is that our consciousness submerges from the wild surface to the stillness of the waters further down. We are not affected by what goes on around. A Tsunami could pass right through and it would make little notable impact on the tranquillity that exists here.

In our waking state, the existence of the day that we perceive, this even-mindedness remains the core of our being. We exist purely in this beingness. Centred, still, untouchable.

You have this inside of you. It just needs enough practiced stillness for it to flourish and become that which you are and always will be. Just being.

It will be there for you, as you, despite what happens around you. It will be your fortress protecting your inner peace, impregnable to the attacks of the mind, to the relentless siege of negative thoughts.

In this way we just accept and let life be.

Events will occur. Life happens.

Thoughts will occur. Mind happens. That is its job.

If an undesirable event occurs, stopping our value of these thoughts, by restriction of our judgements and allowing life to be, can prevent the need for us to experience further such events.

In this way the karmic cycle is broken.

Karma is there to keep reminding us, until we awaken. It will continue to reinforce the teaching, often by increasingly more painful situations, until we learn the lesson that we need to, to be free. Until we see that what is perpetuating, this need for lessons, events and thoughts, is actually just some residual ego upon which the light of consciousness is being shone, like a spotlight it cannot escape from. It is just some part of us that believes itself to be separate from everything else.

This is how the ego is "burned" out of us. It is a fire that must consume everything we 'think' we are.

Once it has destroyed all of that, then what are we? What is left?

What we find is that it is not so much of a discovery, but a remembrance. It is like a person who has been living with Amnesia for many years, suddenly getting a 'total recall'.

Often, we suddenly feel like we did at some point in the past. Possibly a time when we felt completely free.

Our true self.

This feeling of 'just being' is a feeling of being more one's self, than you could have thought yourself to be.

Chapter Twelve

FIGHT THE GOOD FIGHT– GIVING THANKS TO SUFFERING

T HERE ARE TWO WAYS to traverse this path. One involves a lot of hard work, determination, courage, facing fears and delving deep into a kind of peaceful war, where you do not go head-to-head with the mind, as this is a fight you can never win, but you challenge the validity of the thoughts and see them for what they are; devaluing the minds starves it of any chance of success. It's almost likened to an army restricting battle supplies to the enemy, instead of facing it directly on the battlefield.

Another way, often follows the first but can be the chosen path to begin with. It is a complete surrender. It usually occurs when the first way hits a dead end.

When a person gets to a point of utter frustration with a lack of seeming progress, they can often throw it all in. This is of course precisely what is needed at that point and the last part of the journey is done in deepest surrender, of all that remains, to life itself.

When we choose to 'fight the good fight' we have love on our side, we have life on our side. It is not like we can be beaten; the mind cannot beat 'presence', because it exists within it. There for the fights are not fights as we know them, although they may seem like it. But they will repeat until lessons are learned.

Is a war ended in one battle? Most often not. Is a lesson learned in just one teaching? Infrequently. So too the challenge that awaits us all, to overcome the illusion of the ego, is one that is accomplished in many small 'victories'.

You must know that each time you 'catch' the mind causing suffering, you have edged ever closer to freedom from the delusion that ego-mind has created. At this point it is important to rejoice in this and also to be grateful to the grace that has allowed this to be. What is grace? It is the essence of all that is. It is a gift from life to life.

It is very beneficial to give thanks upon witnessing the minds attempts to pull you back in suffering the personal story of the little 'me'.

This will help you, not only to stay on the path, but to shorten the path, out of the darkness of the illusion and into the light.

As you progress along the journey you will notice that the events that continue to cause you suffering will start to be of a similar type. They may also make you feel a certain way or think certain thoughts.

135

What is needed here at first is recognition of the suffering, then enquiry into what it is that caused this.

Start to understand the nature of the events that lead to suffering and also, if possible, try to recall what it was the mind was thinking just prior to the events occurring. Remembering here that our mental projections create the perceived reality we experience. What we repeatedly think, we receive.

Once we are capable of starting to understand what type of thoughts were involved, what type of event took place and what type of suffering occurred (more thoughts/emotions), then we begin to understand what it is that we still need to release from our lives to be free.

It may be that we believe we are 'not enough' and this will create feelings and thoughts of fear, doubt, jealousy etc. These thoughts can at certain times produce events in our perceived 'reality' that will reinforce these feelings/thoughts.

This is the cycle of Karma that continues to hold us in the larger cycle of birth, life and death. One key to dissolving these Samskaras (impressions) that keep us revisiting these types of events is recognition of them, understanding them and beginning to be grateful for them.

This sounds to the mind, completely contradictory. Mind will want you to react, to be fearful, angry at yourself, depressed that it happened again etc. This only helps of course to recreate more of the same.

Instead, we say thanks. We are grateful and give thanks to the event for occurring to show us that which is within us that is binding us to suffering.

It breaks the cycle.

Being grateful for those type of thoughts and events means the ego-mind no longer gets the desired response it needs.

Chapter Thirteen

SURRENDER

F EW WORDS ENCAPSULATE THE essence of spiritual development as much as surrender. As humans we often believe that surrender is a 'giving in' or 'giving up'. Imagining that we are losing power or something else we hold near and dear. We often there for see it as having a very negative connotation.

On this journey though we start to see surrender in its truest form. With freedom from attachment a co-existing practice, we can begin to put into play a type of surrender which now has nothing to lose.

Using acceptance and forgiveness to allow happenings with the knowing that life is presenting to you exactly that which you need to progress. It may be a friend doing something which you feel is offensive that makes you question whether they love you or are right for you. Maybe they didn't even know they had done it or that it would offend you. Life played it out through them in such a way as to make the maximum impact on you. If someone constantly throws rocks at you, use the rocks to build a wall to protect yourself.

It is important that all of the events that challenge your peace arise. For it is then that you can truly learn to hold firm in the belief that you are the 'isness'. How? By seeing time and time again that you are the one that doesn't change. You are there before the event, there during the event and there after the event. You are the same for every event, no matter how challenging, hurtful or painful. Only mind changes. You are the one who witnesses this change.

As soon as you enter the now and stay as isness, all suffering stops. Why? Because it is no longer necessary. Suffering will drive you back home every time. How long is the drive? It depends on how deeply you believe you were ever actually away from home!

So, if we are no longer surrendering anything, then why do we need to?

Surrender works in parallel and as part of the concept of non-attachment. There are many aspects of surrender and all are equally as important on the journey.

The all-encompassing surrender that contains within it all of the other, no less significant surrenders, is the surrender to the now. It can be referred to as surrender to this moment, to the isness of life. Every time we surrender to something, we surrender in essence to this.

Surrender to life is of course also another way of saying we have zero resistance to that which is. Or complete acceptance.

There is no greater practice in which to ease the passage from unconscious to conscious awareness.

Surrendering in this way now becomes an extremely powerful tool, quite the opposite of that which we had believed surrender to be.

Letting go of the need for life to be this way or that way, frees us completely from the jagged edges that may present themselves in our daily activity as the samskaras or karmic actions play out.

We lose our reaction to life.

This is key to breaking free from the karmic cycle.

This will inevitably lead to freedom from suffering as the suffering is in and caused by the reaction process and repeated because of this reaction also. Surrender stops reaction from being possible.

Even if some reaction occurs in the beginning it is witnessed due to the fact that the action is surrendered also.

Without attention, power or belief the reaction is as a sound in a vacuum it has nothing to affect and there for it dissipates very quickly and no ripples occur to cause future similar events, actions and reactions.

If for example you were to stub your toe in a non-surrendered, aggravated or mind active state, you would likely react more than just to the pain in the toe. You would also likely curse the table, yourself, somebody else for moving the table and a whole gamut of thoughts and emotions could then follow such as anger, blame, guilt, regret etc.

However, if you were in state where you had been practicing surrendering to all that is and you did the same thing you would possibly still curse and wince at the pain, but you would remain more as an awareness of the being that stubbed it's toe and there would be a certain disconnect that would prevent any reaction from being a personal one.

In the first event more karmic action would be created to continue the cycle which in turn will lead again to a similar such event which holds the possibility of an unpleasant reaction such as that experienced.

In the latter situation, this cycle is broken as the repetitive karma is exhausted; without need for repeat.

Until we learn to surrender deeply, to all that is, life can feel like it is just a very painful sequence of wash, rinse and repeat.

Chapter Fourteen

FALLING DOWN

WE OFTEN PERCEIVE OURSELVES as 'falling down' again in the spiritual journey of spiritual development. We may begin to be overwhelmed by negative thoughts and subsequent emotions and succumb to the drama by becoming lost in the emotions.

As if the boat of our peaceful self has sailed into tumultuous seas, waves of negative thoughts begin to crash down on us and all may seem lost and out of control.

Often, we can inflame the situation by overreacting to the events we perceive and the feelings we think we are experiencing. We can drive ourselves further into emotional states by reacting to these original emotions in a negative way. We could for example become angrier in a situation creating more regret.

Some people in these extremes of hurtfulness resort to taking alcohol or unprescribed drugs.

These sorts of reactions and responses further drive us away from the clarity of the moment and the truth of the situation.

Here we need to remember that the mind has its own agenda; this is to protect itself from annihilation. It loves drama, as drama helps to create more of a sense of the problematic 'I', 'Me versus the world'.

It often turns to overreacting or mind-altering substances to increase this drive into unconscious behaviour.

To simply be aware of the minds 'wish' is to bring power back away from the mind and focus that power and attention on the true 'self', the one that is aware of the mind. As this power returns, the mind begins to lose its grip and gently begins to dissolve back into awareness itself. Once again, the boat is stabilised and the journey towards the truth of who you are continues.

This failing feeling can occur at any point and at many times along the journey to self-discovery. It may also feel like we are not getting any further or even that we are going backwards instead of progressing.

But here we have to very careful, these thoughts that tell us that we are not doing so well, or not getting better but may actually be getting worse, are coming from the ego-mind. They are self-sabotaging thoughts created to bring back the old belief that 'we are what we think we are' and not that which we are discovering ourselves to be.

Once again, the egoic mind-set launches an assault on your inner peace. Trying to lure it back to the tumultuous seas of chaotic thoughts and beliefs. But it cannot succeed for long, if you keep coming back to that which watches all of this mental activity come and go. You stay right here, in the now as a witness to the thoughts. Here they have no power because they have no attention. They simply just slip away again, like a crocodile back into the murky waters after attacking your boat but not getting what it wants.

If it feels as though an attack has become stronger as the journey progresses then this is just because the subtle things that once made you become emotionally embroiled in mental suffering, no longer have any power over you. The ego-mind targets more complexly threaded issues with the knowing that these will make a stronger impact as they are still widely believed by yourself as part of your *self*.

These tendencies affect you seemingly greater because of the immensity of your belief in their personal attachment. These are often what we would normally call your 'deepest desires'. That which you feel *more deeply*, makes up *more strongly*, that which you believe yourself to be (ego). They invoke the most heightened emotions when thought about. Just a simple thought regarding these ingrained tendencies can sweep you away into endless mind-made imagination and stories, full of emotions such as desire, fear, doubt, anger. Like the character Dorothy in the Wizard of Oz you find yourself whisked away into a seemingly real and all-encompassing story made up by your mind. Full of raw emotions and vividly imagined events, based entirely in the recalled past or imagined future. These intense story-tellings are often enveloped in emotions including desires and fears which can cause a feeling of attraction and aversion. Even when the desire part is acting out mentally, the mind is also often simultaneously creating the opposing negative emotion of fear. This is often seen as desiring an outcome but fearing it not occurring; or desiring to have something but fearing losing it, which often applies to relationships.

Here you can reinforce the tendencies by your emotional reactions to the seemingly real mind-made story being thought out. After it has all finished you may feel a further set of emotions such as guilt or fear. Again, these become attached to the ideology of this tendency.

In this way the egoic self reinforces itself as still 'the one existing'. It makes you not just believe the story, but in doing so it makes you also believe you are the one experiencing the story. Just as in the case of Dorothy, she believes it all to be so true, even though the story playing out is so unrealistic and fantastical.

So how do we put an end to the intense mind play? By realising, just as Dorothy did, that the one controlling the story (in her case the Wizard himself) is nowhere near as powerful as imagined. It is all just trickery; smoke and mirrors. The mind has no power, unless you believe in it. The power is within you, as you. Like Dorothy, who was told at the end that she always had the power, she just had to learn it for herself.

You may not catch yourself during one of these intense creationary stories to begin with but as time goes on and with some of the regular practices mentioned to help find your true self, you will begin to be able to cease the minds trickery even during the midst of one of these very strongly attached believed personal stories.

You continue to be aware of yourself more and more as the witness of all that comes and goes. All is changing when this intense mind activity occurs, except for 'that' which knows it to be changing...be that!

When the egoic-mind can no longer wrestle you away from your peace with even this 'strongest weapon in its arsenal' then it's days of power are truly numbered.

This is the true sign that you are entering the doorway to a higher level of existence, consciousness and bliss.

Holding firm in this awareness of our own simple and unaffected presence we can also begin to overcome even our greatest fears.

Chapter Fifteen

FACING FEARS

I T IS SAID THAT we as human beings are born with only two naturally inherent fears; fear of loud noises and fear of heights. These have been scientifically discovered in humans and found to exist in babies, who are devoid at that point of any other fear. These fears are naturally occurring and probably stem back to creation due to an in-built self-preservation response to life threatening or hazardous situations.

The importance of this knowing lies not so much within the fears we are born with, but the fears that we are born without. If only two fears are natural to us as humans then all of the other fears that we have within us are unnatural and there for created by ourselves.

It is of course quite natural to develop certain fear with regards to safety or personal security such as fear of snakes etc.

But it is also very common to have fears of other things such as particular events happening; an event that you dread and wished would never happen. However constant mindfulness of this fear and the production of the emotions it raises can have the complete opposite effect to that which you desire. If you let the mind and its fear have power over you, it will continue to manifest. Often in this scenario we keep running from thoughts of the fear which means it is never dealt with. This will allow it to perpetuate. It will never go away.

Recognition of our fears is a very empowering action. Accepting that we have fears inside of particular events, which may be something as simple as getting anxiety over being in a room full of people, is the first step towards letting go of something that holds us firmly to our mind-suggested belief of who we are.

One way to overcome and remove these fears to imagine that the event has already occurred. This may be a bit confronting but imagining the event playing out and accepting it is a very powerful tool. By staying present it keeps your mind and emotions steady. Mentally picture it happening and feel that you have accepted it. In this way you can see if you could 'deal with it', if it were to happen. Without all the external stimuli of the event occurring in your senses, you will be in all likelihood very capable of dealing with the situation. Let it play out and witness it happening.

Then once it has played out completely, look at the fear again and see whether it holds power over you still. Or whether if it happens now it actually would not be so bad. Let your heart discover this answer and not your mind. Feel it, don't think it.

Facing our fears in this way helps prevent not only the fear from reoccurring but the likelihood of the event reoccurring. Even if it does, we will fell less vulnerable; distanced from the event in a way in which we witness without attachment.

When we lose our fear for particular events occurring, our mind's influence over creationary occurrence (regarding that particular fear) within our perceived awareness reduces. Which simply means we often get that which we fear most, removing the fear removes that part of the creating potential.

Furthermore, as we free ourselves from the shackles of our fears, we also find ourselves clearing a path towards greater acceptance of 'what is' as our trust and faith in life grows. In this way we also begin to lose our desire for events always to be favourable, which of course always comes with an equal and opposite reaction of fear.

Fear then no longer has a foothold in our existence and it continuously slips away as quickly as it arises, with no ability to grip us any longer.

Freedom from fear is a great step towards freedom from suffering. It breaks the cycle of its self-perpetuating nature of fear-event-more fear.

Removing the fear at the start stops this cycle and assists greatly on the path to true self-realisation.

Remove it by not giving the thoughts of it any power of their own. We do this by limiting the reactivity to fearful thoughts and restricting the belief invested in them.

Chapter Sixteen

RECALLING YOUR POWER

I F GOD (OR ANY other name for the universe creationary force) is the creator of all things, then it stands that this source also created the human mind.

How can it then be that 'gods' will to be free and recognized as consciousness itself is momentarily eclipsed by minds incessant thoughts of otherwise (Ego)? Creating what has been labelled 'Separation consciousness'.

It is almost as though this universal consciousness decided it wanted to play in form and encounter the resistance caused by duality, to encounter the overcoming of such and the returning to oneness, in billions of life forms.

So, if this is the case then Human existence is here to experience both separation (from source) and reunion with source also. How then does perceived separation continue to be, even when consciousness becomes aware of itself?

This that is labelled as 'I', believing itself to be separate to all else, is merely in existence only because it has had an unrealistic amount of belief placed onto it. This is the only thing that keeps it in existence. Yet because it still remains within the existence of consciousness, it cannot exist alone, it has to draw power from somewhere.

This power that keeps your suffering self ever continuing, comes from consciousness itself in the form of your own attention and subsequent belief.

Because the power of god is directed towards mind that is the only way it can have any power of its own.

Unplug the mind from the power of god.

Don't give it any attention.

Stop believing what your mind tells you to be true. Start to see that the truth alone exists continuously in that in which the mind is simply witnessed; Conscious awareness itself.

Removing the power from the mind made self-image, will gradually remove all that you perceive to be that which suffers life. What will remain is the life itself, you will not be separate from this.

Here, life will look after life. It will be smoother. Like a gentle flowing river.

If all that is experienced is within this field of universal consciousness, then soon enough it will all merge as one.

Without separation, there is no suffering.

Understanding that your self is the same as any other self that exists including that of any divine creator/ creationary life force or even life itself.

There is great power in this. Not a personal power that makes you feel I am very powerful or have more power than others; but an inner creationary power that instils a sense of confidence, peace and trust in life.

By finding your self you can find an unending source of self-empowerment.

You begin to notice that this power that exists within, focussed and directed with attention, is very important to overcoming any perceived potential vulnerability to the naturally occurring events of life.

Chapter Seventeen

SELF-
EMPOWERMENT

Y OU ARE THE ONLY one that can make you feel anything.

You are the only one that can make you feel unhappy, fearful, angry, jealous, envious, suicidal. All of these and all other feelings inside come from you, to you.

Look inside and see if this is true.

How does this idea make you feel? Sit with it for a moment and really feel how this makes you feel.

Does it make you feel hatred towards your self for making you 'go through' everything you go through?

If it does then sit with that feeling also.

Is that not also just another feeling you are imposing upon yourself to make you feel even more 'against life'?

Again, just sit with this and let this new concept 'wash' over you. Let it just be.

Another thought that may arise from this powerful idea, is that you may feel that it is not possible for you to stop these feelings.

Let us stop again for a moment and have a look at this.

Just think, we are responsible for our own feelings.

You may start to notice that the instead of feeling opposed to this concept you begin to notice that it has a certain essence of optimism within it. It can begin to feel that instead of being a hopeless victim to life's ability to make you feel this or that. You start to feel that you are in charge.

You have the say over how you feel. Nobody, no event, no words, no situation can make you 'feel' any feelings and emotions. It is all you. An example of this is that some people like classical music, it makes them feel incredibly happy, they may get goose-bumps, tears of joy. Yet another person listens to the same music and it grates them, makes them agitated, depressed or want to run. Same music, different people.

We have a choice. We have the ultimate choice. All of the power is within you. It is yours always. It always has been.

You get to feel how you want to feel.

Does this mean you can always be happy? Initially probably not. But yes, it does and can and will.

It also means that you do not have keep going on suffering from the painful feelings, you impose upon yourself.

Taking responsibility for the fact that it is you own egoic mind, the self you believe you are, that makes you suffer instead of others or life itself is one of the fastest ways to come to the complete annihilation of not only the suffering of this mind, this ego, this false self and subsequently all of this suffering. It is like morphine for your soul. Pain free.

Stop looking outside of your self for reasons why you are unhappy. Do not look to blame others for how you feel. That does not mean anyone has the right to treat you unfairly or to abuse you but if they do it is your choice as to how you deal with it. That is empowerment of the highest level.

If life throws you a 'curve ball' and you feel as though you have had a rough time of late or a troubled past, then look inside to what 'feels' that. Is it your mind keeping its own perceptions of how things should have been as opposed to how they turned out? Was it life that made you miserable, or yourself?

When you stop still for a few moments and enquire within yourself, you will find your answer. Stillness gives you the ability to see beyond thoughts.

Look deep inside yourself and know that you are that which knows that. The perceiver.

Take strength in this understanding.

Allow your existence to stem from this place. Empowered. Free from events and actions. Free from self-imposed suffering.

This may happen instantly or it may take time. But remember if it takes time, it is just the mind that is making it take time by offering up a challenge to that which you have discovered in your own truth. It is ok. Just be in your being-ness. All will be well.

It is probably a good point here to remember that you must also be cautious of a sense of self that is either going well or going very slowly on the path to awareness of your truth. Either is created once again by the egoic mind to maintain a sense of false self. Even if it is a flurry of thoughts praising how far you have come, this is still a very limiting factor. It is still creating a you that is mind made.

Likewise, the mind can turn on the sense of self with negative commentary. Again, it is perpetuating itself with thoughts and subsequent belief.

Chapter Eighteen

SPIRITUAL SEEKER - THE FALSE WITNESS

A LONG THE PATH OF self-seeking, one can come to a point in which it feels as though you have achieved so much and yet it just never seems to be enough. You have come so far and had so many realisations but yet the bridge always seems to get a bit longer every time you are near the other side.

This is a very common occurrence.

What is occurring here is that the one who believes himself to be a spiritual seeker or one looking for enlightenment or awakening, is also part of the mind-made sense of self and must also be let go.

Seeing yourself as a spiritual seeker is of course much better than seeing yourself as many other things, but it can also be a belief of who you are which is a very strong illusion created by reinforced values of 'a better you'.

As we follow a path towards finding our self, we quite often have many small and even some large successes towards finding peace within. What we need to steer clear of, which can be a challenge at the beginning, is to create another perspective of our self which is this time a spiritually evolved person.

Yes, it is good to be grateful and allow the confidence to grow as we begin to finally transform what may have been a self with a great deal of suffering and lack of self-confidence, but it must not be replaced by an opposite ego that takes all of this credit for itself and begins to see itself as higher than others, deserving of more or spiritually evolved.

What is needed is to view life again as a natural flow, in a way in which we see all that comes to us as a grace and naturally flowing from life into the life that we are. In this way we ourselves are removed. Life takes care of life.

Then whatever occurs, be it a sudden and great transformation or a slow and steady awareness of a self which is more present and less person, it is all just allowed to be. We once again go along for the ride, a passenger, so to speak.

This way our ego is not replaced and the self that we find re-emerging is not contaminated or reliant on any outcomes.

Great vigilance is required here because as the ego-mind finds that it has less and less to cling to in its efforts to maintain itself, so too will it look for more and more subtle ways to achieve this.

In this way we can start to believe that we are seeing our self for who we truly are but what we truly are cannot ever be seen, so even this is a false sense of self. What we truly are simply just is. It can be experienced as our self, but cannot be described.

This is a very good example of how any doing or achieving that we believe to occur unto our self is laced with the poison of attachment. Here we puff our chest up a bit and say this is what I have done, how far I have come and what is mine that I can never lose. The ego-mind loves to believe that it is constantly achieving new things to have more or be better and so too can it do the same with regards to spiritual evolvement.

The truth is that we have not gained anything, in fact we have lost much. We have lost or are losing all that we are not. All that we have gained is a recollection or rediscovering of that which we truly are, in our essence.

Constant remembrance of this and the fact that our true self needs nothing (no thing) to be, will help to surrender any achievements or accept them without ownership as 'the doer'. Freeing us once again from any mind made sense of self.

The ability to create this continued sense of self awareness is what is known as presence. Being present in this moment is something that can simply be achieved and yet holds such immense power. Life is present. Creation itself is present. You are also always present. They are all one and the same.

Chapter Nineteen

STAYING PRESENT

THE KEY TO INNER stillness is being fully present with a relaxed but focussed attention towards the witnessing consciousness you are.

If you sit for a moment, any moment, even if just for 5 seconds and watch the world around you, you will inevitably notice things change. It may be that you are inside and you can hear a clock tick, or see bubbles rise around playing fish in a tank, it may be just as subtle as slight changes in your breath or fine dust particles moving through a ray of sunlight coming through a window.

Alternatively, you could be outside and as you pause for just a few seconds you see a slight breeze move the grass or leaves on a tree. A dog may bark or a car pass in the distance. Clouds may very slowly move across the sky.

Even if you were to sit in a pitch dark, sound proof room alone, you would still be aware of your heart beating once more, a new breath, another thought.

So just even in just a very small time period, many changes can be witnessed.

'Life' itself is created by change. We are born, we grow, we experience different things and we die. That is what we have determined to be 'a life'.

Yet still, with all this that is changing, something remains behind it all, changeless. A witnessing consciousness without which you would not be able to be aware of the change.

As the cloud crossing the sky does not affect the sky. Then all of the activities that occur within your conscious awareness do not affect that which you are. Still and silent, as the cloudless sky.

This is the key to meditation and the practices that have occurred for many thousands of years regarding this search for inner stillness. But not just meditation; more importantly this is the key to freedom from suffering also to life itself.

Once you can become this still, present awareness during changes, you will soon master the ability to remain still and present during all of life, including those events which may be classified as upheavals or challenges.

Then life no longer seems so challenging, confronting or unfair. It simply is, because you let it be.

The way to maintain this stillness is to keep bringing the focussed awareness back away from that which is changing to that which does not. It is as simple as that.

In this way, you will not only learn that you are more this still and present conscious awareness than anything else you ever thought yourself to be, but you will also begin to feel the blissfulness that emanates from it into all of the life that plays out.

To begin with it may take a bit of effort to maintain this withdrawal of your focussed attention from the seeming distractions of external events and minds interpretations, but as time goes on it will become an effortless practice.

As you find yourself more and more in this state of inner peace, with attention withdrawn from minds activities and that of the senses, you will begin to discover the easiness of staying present in life's ever-changing situations. You will not fall for the old trap of following the mind on some adventure into past or future and wild imaginings. Instead, you will be still, fully present in the now. Ignoring any impulses to get lost in thought or judgements of events and ongoings. You will develop an inner awareness that subtly challenges and prevents overthinking. Mind will still be used to assess, but not empowered to govern events.

Here you will stay. Present in this moment. A deep inner peace and stillness. Experiencing more of life than you may have thought possible. Not just living life, but being it. One with it. Such presence; such peace; such stillness; such blissful joy.

Chapter Twenty

TRUE LOVE
– ONENESS

THE WORD NAMASTE MEANS "I salute the place in you, where you and I are one". It is a way of acknowledging that the true self you are, is no different to the true self of any other; this is oneness. You find yourself in others and others in your own self. This is something that my master Swamiji often pointed towards as a phenomenon that would occur more and more as you progress along the journey.

It is not only a beautiful form of respect and greeting. It is also an acceptance and confirmation that although there are differences in ourselves on a physical material level, below all that we can perceive we are actually one and the same. This helps to remove not just the blocks that exist between 'us and others' but it also helps to bring us in line with the play of existence, by aligning us and our needs with those of all we meet.

Although as you continue your journey it is likely that this natural connection will occur it is also possible to initiate this your self.

Making a deep connection with another, be it another Human or even a pet or other animal, is possibly something that you have already experienced in your life. It is a beautiful moment in which the world around seems to dull in distraction leaving only the two parties involved in importance of existence. It is often a silent moment and a knowing exists that something is there, a bond, that cannot be seen or heard or barely even talked about. It just is.

This connection is often surprising as it is far greater than the imagined existing relationship bond of which we are normally aware. Its depth is unparalleled.

It is also something that if we have not achieved can be fairly easily experienced by finding another being and just allowing yourself to just be around them. This may be anything living; a goldfish, tree, dog or even another person.

Very peaceful animals such as cats are often the best animals to begin with or experience this. They, like most animals, are very good at being fully present in the moment and just being themselves.

What is necessary however for us to experience oneness is to also bring about these abilities in ourselves; we must be fully present and have no self judgement. This means do not label yourself or take on any role. Just be present as your self in the moment; Fully.

Making this type of connection with others is so beneficial to your journey. Firstly, it enables you to be you, without anything added. Which feels both wonderfully empowering and freeing all at the same time. Also, it allows the other the opportunity to witness exactly the same. It is almost as though with no self-imposed image you each hold up a mirror to each other in which nothing exists expect the no-thingness you each portray.

Secondly, it enables your self to be more open to the natural flow of life, which in turn brings about less suffering, by holding at the core of your being a knowing that you and others (especially fellow humans) are nothing but one and the same. This removes feelings such as unworthiness, jealousy, anger etc.

Imagine, as John Lennon said, what a world like this would feel like?

Being able to see your self in others and others in your own self, this is true compassion, true love. Not just the love that is formed by romantic or caring feelings, but a deeper love. One which negates a 'yourself and another', it removes the I/me and you. It leaves a connection even greater than us or we. Words in fact fail here to describe this connection; as it is something we have not really had to do.

Finding your self is of great importance; it has no parallel in as far as opening up to a life free from suffering. Finding yourself in another; this enables the true essence that is within us all to emanate out and light up the lives of not just our self but all else. In this way we begin to see that there is only the one life, existing in all living things.

When we come to this realisation, life simply unfolds, beautifully. Almost magically. No longer a struggle; we are free from suffering. We know our Self to **be** one with life and all that is. Simple. Blissful. Eternal.

GLOSSARY

Atman - The true self or inner self. Referring to pure consciousness or witness-consciousness, beyond identification with phenomena.

Bhagavad Gita - A sacred Hindu text composed between fifth century to the second century B.C.E.

Buddha – A Sanskrit word that translates to "Enlightened or Awakened". Usually referring to Siddhārtha Gautama a prince and religious leader and teacher who lived in ancient India (c. 6th to 4th century B.C.E). Founder of Buddhism.

Ego - The individual's sense of who they are – their thoughts, desires and personality, as shaped by the mind.

Ego-mind – The false self or the conditioned mind. A state of lack of conscious awareness (unconsciousness) where we are constantly identified with our thoughts and emotions, reactions, desires, and aversions.

Guna – A Sanskrit word meaning a 'Quality'. In Hinduism there are three Gunas, being sattva, rajas and tamas. Each having different qualities and producing different tendencies. All things have a different proportion of each.

Karma/Karmic/Karmic cycle – Karma is a Sanskrit word that means action, deed and intent. Referring to the spiritual principle of cause and effect. This Causality decrees that executed actions and intentions of an individual affects the individual and the life he or she lives. The karmic cycle is the constant playing out of event - reaction to event (action with intent) - further similar events.

Maya – A Sanskrit word – usually translated as 'Illusion'. The illusion that the world is as it appears to be and all of its distractions. Maya is the illusion of existence in duality and of separation of self from all else.

Moksha – A Sanskrit word meaning "Freedom or Liberation". Referring to freedom from the suffering cycle of death and rebirth by knowledge of Atman and the subsequent release from the suffering of the egoic mind and the illusion of Maya.

Namaste – A Sanskrit derived word, Namasté is a traditional Indian greeting of respect and reverence. It is also used a salutation to recognise one's self in others and others in oneself, with the translation 'I bow to the place in you where we are both one'.

Om symbol – A Sacred symbol first seen in ancient texts which signifies Ultimate Reality, symbolising the various states of consciousness and the illusion of any other perceived reality.

Samskaras (also Sanskaras) – Stored impressions caused by action or intent, which manifest as tendencies and karmic impulses. In Buddhism it is believed that they should be purified and not necessarily eliminated.

Sanskrit – A classical ancient language of South Asia first recorded around 1500 B.C.E.

Sattva/Sattvic – Sattva is one of the three *Gunas*. It is the tendency towards and/or the quality of balance, harmony, goodness, peace and creativity. A 'Sattvic' lifestyle promotes purity within by following a sattvic diet and healthy spiritual practices.

Turiya – Pure Consciousness. That state which underlies the three other states of consciousness; being the waking, dreaming sleep and dreamless deep-sleep states. It is a state of union also referred to as conscious Samadhi.

Upekkhā – A Pali language word which translates as the Buddhist concept of equanimity. It is Even-mindedness and the ability to be calm and balanced, especially in the midst of difficulty.

Impermanence - The state or fact of lasting for only a limited period of time. Also, a Buddhist philosophy that all existence is temporary. All events, both physically and mentally perceived are not constant or permanent; coming to into being and then dissolving.

Meditation - A practice in which a technique such as mindfulness or body awareness, is used to train attention and become aware of (and resting peacefully in) awareness itself, which observes mental activity without attachment.

Conscious awareness – The state of being aware of your self as consciousness. Achieved often by meditation and focussing attention on that conscious state which exists beyond, yet also encompasses, the activities of the mind.

Yogi – A person who practices *yoga*.

Yogic/Yoga – A Sanskrit word meaning 'Yoke' or "Union". Practices originating in ancient India which are aimed at recognizing a detached witness-consciousness untouched by the mind (Atman). Evolving beyond the illusion of an individual self (*ego*) and realising union with the divine self (*God*).

Separation consciousness – A mentally created illusory belief that we are separate from all else. A from of *Maya* and complete lack of realisation of our self as *Atman*.

Enlightenment/spiritually awakened – The realisation and continued awareness of our self as Consciousness, free from *Ego*.

Master/Guru – A person often referred to as a spiritual teacher, who has become spiritually awakened and passes on this wisdom to other seekers. Often sharing events and realisations of their own self-discovery journey to act as 'sign-posts' for others to follow.

Riptide - A strong current pulling towards the sea.

Consciousness – A state of higher awareness that transcends the mind.

God – A spirit or being believed to create life and the universe. Often synonymous with Brahman (or Absolute Reality) it can also refer to a Supreme Consciousness, of which human consciousness is both part of and as one with.

AFTERWORD

OFTEN PEOPLE HAVE ASKED me how the name 'The White Cat' was chosen for the title of such a book. There are two reasons, one of which symbolises the essence of the book and the other highlights one of the rewards of this essence.

Eckhart Tolle famously said: "I have lived with several Zen masters – all of them cats".

Throughout my spiritual journey, I was often surrounded by many cats as our families' pet of choice. Many times, over the years with different cats, I noticed the stillness of which Tolle referred too.

One particular white cat, called 'Luna', belonging to my young daughter. This cat had an incredible ability to allow all that occurred, with a surrendered temperament that seemed at one with life, no matter what occurred. I would often walk into my daughter's room and find the cat covered in a variety of objects, dressed in cat costumes or being gently physically pushed, poked or moved. Regardless of what this young girl lovingly did to her nonchalant pet, Luna just sat and allowed it all to occur.

Coming back night and night again to simply 'be' with her young owner.

It occurred to me at that point that out of all the cats, this one epitomised the essence of my learnings and acquired wisdom on the spiritual journey.

The other reason for the naming of this book, has to do with a particular phrase "The Black Dog" which is often used to symbolise and refer to Depression.

Having personally experienced depression, it occurred to me that it was at these times when my sense of a mind made self was strong. Depression having a very strong capability of creating personalised suffering, increasing the belief in an illusory mentally created concept of self (Ego).

This was the extreme opposite of the essence of the book and it seemed fitting that the book be called something that was also quite the opposite of 'The Black Dog'.

Having the ability to separate the self from physical or mental suffering, including depression, is one of the rewards of the journey.

I hope, with all my heart, that you also find this freedom from suffering.

Dave Musson

PERSONAL NOTES